Praise for *Unbinding the Soul*

Unbinding the Soul enables [readers] to achieve self-transformation, while developing compassion for themselves . . . offering tools to expand mind-body awareness and release from fear and negative attachments.

— Gloria Arenson, MFT, DCEP
Author of *Five Simple Steps to Emotional Healing*

[A] compelling journey through personal transformation . . . through darkness and pain that can open us to deep compassion. Reach for the light in the darkness, as you gather the courage to heal your soul.

— Dawn Lianna MA, NLP
Author of *The 8 Keys to Powerful Intuition*

Copyright © 2015 Dr B. Raven Lee
All rights reserved.

ISBN: 1508952396
ISBN 13: 9781508952398

Unbinding the Soul

Awakening Through Crisis and Compassion

DR B. RAVEN LEE

Dedicated to

My root lama, Tenzin Wangyal Rinpoche,
My Bön teachers and sangha,
Tomás, Randy, Jennifer and family,
My students,
And to all those who have entrusted me to help them
Unbind their Souls

TABLE OF CONTENTS

Foreword ix
Acknowledgments xi
Introduction xv

PART I – THE VIEW
1. The Fire of Initiation 3
2. The Journey of the Self 19
3. Shattered Illusions 48

PART II – THE PATH
4. Radiant Heart – The Healing Power of Compassion 75
5. Mindful Listening – The Wisdom of Turning Inward 89
6. Riding the Waves of Emotion: Integration towards Wholeness 104
7. The Heart-Mind Transformation Process: An Integrated Approach 127

PART III – THE FRUITION
8. The Dance of Awareness 143
9. Beyond Hope and Fear 165

APPENDIX I – The Triune Brain 183
APPENDIX II – The Nine Domains of Integration 187
REFERENCES 189
INDEX 193

FOREWORD

Raven Lee has been a dedicated student of mine for quite some time. She has received the teachings of the Bön lineage with an open heart and applies them to her own life in a way that is genuine and fearless. I have witnessed much transformation in her and trust her as a senior teacher in The 3 Doors, a contemplative, secular non-profit organization dedicated to bringing the essence of the Bön teachings to many in a simple and accessible way for personal and social transformation.

Raven has a sincere motivation that her own healing be of benefit for others. By expressing her own journey through suffering, along with her knowledge in the fields of psychology, science, and spirituality, Raven articulates and illuminates a simple message: opening to our own suffering can be a powerful door to transformation and become a path of healing and benefit for oneself and others.

This is a wonderful book and I am sure it will help many people.

Tenzin Wangyal Rinpoche
California USA
March 10, 2015

ACKNOWLEDGMENTS

This book is a fruition of almost three decades of transformation, learning and integration on a personal, professional, and community level. There were many moments of riding the waves of doubts about the message I received to share this journey of unbinding our souls.

I wish to acknowledge first and foremost my Bön lineage and teachers, whose authentic warmth and wisdom inspired me to keep dissolving the effort and write from joy and an open heart.

There were countless others who became part of the soul of this manifestation. From the moment I received the title and wrote down the bones of the story, Dr. Naomi Serrano, a wise woman, healer and beloved friend, became my staunchest supporter and encouraged me to obtain my doctorate and transform this story into my dissertation. Though she has since crossed over, Naomi remains as an angel in my heart. I would also like to thank Dr. Inula Martinkat, my dissertation advisor, for her guidance and support.

I have a heartfelt gratitude to my mother-in-law, Elaine Ward for her belief in the inner realm and the magic of storytelling. Her generous sponsorship enabled me to take time off from my work and devote it to birthing this book.

To my sacred circle of spiritual sisters and healers: Elizabeth Sloane, whose unwavering belief in my message and our friendship became a flame that kept the book alive. I am grateful for our enlivening dialogues about sacred feminine and the shadow. Dr. Eileen Kenny, who would 'put me back together' after each peek and blast into the spectrum of consciousness since 1987. She continues to integrate my dimensional jet lags. Marie-Jeanne, whose journey of courage amid doubts and fear, is a symbol of the path to awakening. I cherish our playful friendship that spanned over three decades. Jeannie Kang, whose radiant heart and support nourishes my soul. And I would also like to thank my Wellness Institute sisters, Becky, Lisa, Celedra, and Reatha.

I would like to express my heartfelt gratitude to all my other teachers and mentors, especially Maud Ann Taylor, Linda Garbett and Terumichi, for their love and wisdom.

To Paul and Roy for their love and support through the meanderings of my journey of awakening.

I give thanks to all my patients whose descent into their abyss became the gifts of their awakening. Their courage and trust in the process reflect the power of compassionate wisdom and open awareness. I am humbled and honored to be their guide and witness along their journeys of transformation.

Also, I would like to thank all those who read earlier versions of the manuscript, offered their feedback, editing skills, and encouragement. I especially would like to acknowledge Jan Friebergs, my spiritual sister and healer, who read the first draft in 1995, and has since followed my labyrinthine path, and Stephanie Marohn, whose 'editing eye' kept pointing me to the fruition.

Words cannot describe my profound gratitude to Janet Ciccarelli Lucas, my senior student and spiritual sister, for her dedication, expertise in editing, subtle hearing and gnosis of what I was trying to convey. I rejoice in the countless hours of dialoguing and editing at the Parkway Grill restaurant, supported by the loving attention of Kevin, who knew how to serve not only gastronomic nourishment, but also our need for silence.

A special thanks goes to Janine Vigus for her patience and her expert work designing the beautiful cover of this book. Her artistic sensibility immediately intuited what I had in mind. I would also like to thank Jonathan Chang for providing the beautiful Chinese calligraphy of the characters for *crisis, opportunity* and *listen*.

ACKNOWLEDGMENTS

I give thanks to my students, the Dragonfly tribe in southern California, and the Coarse community in southern France, who have learned that suffering is a crack in the doorway to awaken the Light of our Souls, and are now sharing this message while becoming Vessels of Light.

I would like to express my deep gratitude to my parents and my siblings, Gladys and Randolph, who knew me first as Barbara, and witnessed the long years of my transformation. Though puzzled at times about my strange encounters, their love for me is palpable. To my children, Randy and Jennifer, who have taught me so much about the mystery of love and the jewel in the ordinariness of our human existence, my gratitude knows no limits.

Lastly, I wish to acknowledge Tomás, my soul mate, my mirror, my sounding board, my editor-in-chief, my advisor, who urged me never to give up, keeps me laughing and loves me with all his heart and soul.

INTRODUCTION

The sole purpose of human existence is to kindle a light in the darkness of mere being.
C. G. Jung

Trust your wounds . . . they are where the light can enter.
Rumi

Anyone who has suffered knows the meaning of the phrase, *darkness of mere being*. The psychological wounds of our past and the uncertainties of our human existence contribute to an underlying fear and vulnerability, which become magnified and consume us when we are thrown into crisis. Our adaptation skills shattered, we find ourselves adrift in a sea of confusion. In the darkness of our suffering, we lose the light that shows us the way through. Jung's light, *the sole purpose of our existence*, comes not from the outer world, but arises from our innate awareness of oneness, the *Light of our Divine Spark*. As the great poet, Rumi suggests in the opening quote, our wounds offer a doorway to reconnect with our divine spark, a light that is filled with loving compassion and wisdom, a beacon that brings meaning to our suffering and returns us to our True Self.

By shining a light in the darkness we can begin the difficult but rewarding process of transforming suffering into wisdom, a process I know well. Within the darkness of my own crisis, I experienced a kindling of radiant light filled with a pervasive compassionate presence that transformed my fearful mind into a mind filled with deep peace and unconditional love. My awakening called me to search for the causes of suffering, the path of healing, and the nature of enlightened mind.

Crisis forces us to pause, uncertain of how to respond to, feel or experience life. In an instant, our capacity to cope and make sense of reality becomes inadequate. Brought to our knees with nowhere external to turn to for solutions, we must look inward and discover our own inner light. This encapsulates the meaning of the title, *Unbinding the Soul*. Crisis can awaken us to the light of *compassionate awareness,* penetrating our innermost beings, and unbinding our essence. This means loosening and relaxing the ties that bind us to our ego identity, preventing us from being in the present moment, a moment that opens us to the essence that resides within all of us. Deep healing can begin when the fearful and vulnerable aspects of our selves are supported by a greater presence, a compassionate awareness, like that of a mother soothing her frightened child.

Over almost three decades, I immersed myself in discovering a therapeutic model to guide and support my patients, who often sought help because of a crisis. What seemed impossible or improbable at the beginning of therapy – that these deep wounds could be healed – came to fruition before our eyes. As my patients grew stronger in their ability to witness and experience their emotional pain, they were able to access the transformative power of the *compassionate observer* in navigating the labyrinth of their suffering. The compassionate observer is the ultimate guide who takes us by the hand and shines a light as we stumble through the darkness. This model of healing, or *unbinding the soul,* is a step-by-step process that teaches us how to embrace the crises and suffering of our human existence.

Central to this model is the cultivation of *compassionate awareness* as the unbreakable container for our frenzied, fearful aspects, which can be transformed into wisdom and strength. This book teaches one how to develop the compassionate awareness that is kind, gentle, and wise beyond words. This process of healing, both as participant and guide, is beautiful to behold.

INTRODUCTION

Though the steps of the process may appear simple, the journey from darkness to light is not easy, as you will learn from my own story. The journey, which is never straightforward or linear, requires dedicated effort, involving many missteps and wrong turns. In fact, our missteps and wrong turns are what lead us to our own awakening. It does not matter how long the journey takes; what matters is that you *begin the journey.*

No one can predict where your journey will lead. Had anyone told me that my journey of awakening would eventually lead to my becoming a mystic shaman healer and spiritual teacher, I would have laughed, and said, "You got to be joking!" Little from my background indicated such a calling. Yet, this is where my journey led me. At the time of my crisis, I had no way to know that my suffering would crack me open, unlocking the doors of awareness, unbinding my soul and lighting my path to become a mystic shaman healer.

When I reflect on my past, nothing in my childhood prepared me for the life of a healer. I was born and grew up in a neighborhood called Happy Valley, in Hong Kong, which sounds idyllic but was not for me. Raised as a traditional Chinese Catholic, I was shy, insecure, fearful, and prone to anxiety and depression. My family and my childhood religious training molded me into a conservative, subservient young girl. I learned this role and I played it to perfection. It seems incredulous to me now, that this anxious young girl would eventually grow up to become a powerful spiritual healer, completely confident in her abilities. Yet is this not the wondrous mystery we all seek to realize, that within our ordinariness and darkness of mere being, there is a profound purpose and sacredness? What awakened me to my calling as a mystic shaman healer was a severe crisis that kindled the light and propelled me on a quest.

Although it feels like yesterday, my crisis happened in 1985. By then, I had been married for almost a decade to a man whose quiet, controlled moods I had mistaken as signs of stability and security. I met my husband when I came to United States to begin graduate studies in clinical social work. My early training as a dutiful daughter prepared me to be the subservient young wife, who deferred to her dominant husband. As I began to find my voice and challenge my sheltered, protected life as a dutiful housewife, my husband had a psychotic breakdown. After many traumatic encounters, he committed suicide.

Widowed with two young children, I was completely overwhelmed by despair, shame and guilt. Everything that I had learned as a child seemed to come tumbling down like a ton of bricks. I had always believed that doing the right thing would be rewarded with safety, comfort and stability. However, there is no safety or comfort when sharing a home with someone who is experiencing violent, psychotic episodes. Nothing from my childhood prepared me for coping or understanding such a devastating and seemingly senseless tragedy.

Teetering on the edge of insanity, I felt desperate for an answer to my suffering. The answer came through a dear friend, whose introduction to a spiritual healer led me to my first experience of an expanded awareness. While being guided in deep meditation I encountered a bright light, the very light of Jung and Rumi. Entering into a sacred space, my deep trauma filled with compassionate awareness, I experienced total peace. The heaviness and confusion I felt from my crisis instantly dissolved. I sensed something great and wise burst forth from within me, an aspect of myself that was ageless, joyous and boundless. I was one with the universe, filled with unconditional love and compassion, including compassion for the part of me that was deep in crisis. Spontaneously, from beyond my thinking mind, I 'knew' the meaning of suffering and the purpose of human existence. My awakening marked the beginning of my journey home to my True Self, my authentic essence.

The week following this transcendent experience, I remained in a state of bliss. The anxious widowed mother within me felt held in a loving embrace. Experiences that previously had thrown me into fits of anger – my children's constant bickering or their refusal to do homework – no longer rattled me. My mind felt clear and calm. Disturbing thoughts and negative emotions arose and then dissolved like puffs of clouds in the blue spacious sky. I felt grounded and joyful, untouched by the swirling commotion that surrounded me.

My bliss, however, did not last. A week later, after a particularly demanding day at work, my sense of calm came to an abrupt end. While attempting to break up a fight between my son, Randy, and my daughter, Jennifer, I completely lost my connection to the light of compassionate awareness. Separated from love and peace, I succumbed to the darkness. In a fit of anger, I found myself screaming at my children. Immediately after, I felt disappointment and disgust, asking myself, "What kind of mother are you?" Doubts circled my head, spiraling me into a pit of guilt and despair. The clarity and joy I had known the previous week was shattered, replaced with a constricted and harshly critical 'self' that judged me a monstrous mother.

Negative thoughts consumed me. Gone was the compassionate awareness that had emerged from my encounter with my spiritual healer. Yet the light of my awakening hadn't been completely extinguished, merely obscured by stress. After a few days of darkness, a loving energy began to stir within my heart. The overwhelming waves of darkness subsided, and my doubts of being a good mother dissolved into a vast vibration of compassion. Awed by this transformative experience, I craved to learn how to stabilize it, to integrate the compassionate awareness, the light of awakening, the calm, the bliss, and the joy into my daily life and into the deepest aspects of my being.

After my awakening, I immersed myself in Jung's writings, intent on becoming a Jungian analyst. But destiny had a different plan. A series of powerful, initiatory dreams revealed that I was to follow another path. In one dream, a voice declared that I would become a shaman healer. With much trepidation and even more reluctance, I finally accepted what my dreams had foretold. Whether I liked it or not, I was called to become a mystic shaman healer.

Before accepting my new role I would need to gain much knowledge and experience. I wanted to understand energy and matter. I wanted to know higher states of consciousness and experience them for myself. In addition to my shamanic training, I delved into other fields of knowledge, including Jung's archetypes, Taoism, Qi Gong, Buddhism, quantum mechanics, energy psychology and interpersonal neurobiology. I reconnected with my Catholic roots and explored Mystical Christianity and Gnosticism. My shamanic training transformed my perspective, allowing me to experience the infinite cosmic web that weaves innumerable dimensions and spirit worlds. These thrill rides into alternate realms of consciousness were always paired with a pervasive, compassionate wisdom, which was the heart of my meditation practice and my devotion to mystic and Buddhist teachings.

My awareness expanded further when I discovered Bön, the indigenous religion of Tibet. I was excited to learn that Bön encompasses shamanic practices and Dzögchen, the highest level of realization, passed on through an oral tradition from teacher to student (see Chapter 9). Central to the Bön teachings is awakening to our innate essence. My root lama or main teacher, Tenzin Wangyal Rinpoche introduced me to the nature of mind, which is another name for this essence. The formal Bön teachings solidified my experiential learning, which in turn deepened my meditation practice. I quickly noticed changes in my thoughts and emotions, which led to significant changes in my behavior.

I shared my new perspective with my closest friend. "My awareness is different and my brain is not the same. I am looking at life through new lenses." As I learned later, science had demonstrated the positive effects of meditation and spiritual experiences on the brain and body. Intrigued by the mind/body/spirit connection, I explored the frontiers between spirituality and science, earning a doctorate in Transpersonal Psychology. For someone with no previous interest in science, I became enamored with the study of quantum physics and neurobiology. Science confirmed what I had intuited -- we are biologically hardwired to communicate, connect, and evolve to higher states of consciousness.

As I explored and integrated these different disciplines, I discovered doorways into the mystical realms, first descending into the darkness of the epic human story, and then harnessing its healing energy and transforming psychic wounds. By applying the gifts I had learned in my therapeutic practice, I found that I could help my patients cultivate a unique kind of awareness and connection. I enabled them to awaken an inner light and heal themselves. Having experienced how crisis and suffering can be doorways to transformation, I felt deeply compelled to share my journey of healing with others, and thus, the birthing of this book.

INTRODUCTION

INSPIRATION FOR THE TITLE OF THE BOOK

In 1988, three years after my husband's suicide, my quest to understand my powerful awakening took me to the tranquil and idyllic village of Kushnacht, Switzerland, site of the C.G. Jung Institute. I went there to pay homage to the master. As I sat on the couch in the break room, housed in the basement of its main building, out of nowhere I heard the words, *"Unbinding the Soul. This is the book you are to write."* Accompanying these words were images of countless contorted faces writhing in pain, unable to speak or move. I was shaken by this revelation. I emerged from the basement trembling with anticipation and apprehension. The title given me was intimidating, and the idea of writing a book was extremely daunting.

What does *unbinding the soul* mean? What is the nature of a soul that needs unbinding? The title itself became a daily reflection and my holy grail. Although I was raised Catholic, I did not understand the meaning of *soul*, nor was it a concept explored in my early education in psychology. I was trained in the scientific study of mind, but the concept of *soul* was rarely discussed, much less defined. Despite religion's and psychology's longtime dedicated interest in understanding the *soul*, the concept has eluded precise definition; perhaps because the very nature of *soul* is ineffable.

In the 1800s, Western psychology began as the study of the psyche, or *soul*. In 1835, its founding father, Gustav Fechner, who claimed an ability to quantify the mind using experimental observation and empirical studies, wrote of a higher spiritual life that "lies hidden in every human mind."[1] At the heart of Fechner's thesis is what he called the 'divine germ' of consciousness. This divine germ or seed enables humans to evolve from a physical body into the realm of the mind and spirit. William James, still considered the most influential psychologist of the 19th century, noted that 'our normal waking consciousness,' or rational consciousness, is only one of many forms of consciousness.

---

[1] Fechner, G. *The Little Book of Life After Death*, 1904. Also read Hawkins, S. *William James, Gustav Fechner, and early Psychophysics*, 2011.

James theorized that if we "apply the requisite stimulus" to the mind, other potential forms of consciousness would appear.[2]

Thirty years before Freud, Karl Robert Eduard von Hartmann, author of *The Philosophy of the Unconscious*, wrote about the existence of a cosmic consciousness, which when fully realized was humankind's 'greatest good.' Greatly influenced by von Hartman, Jung proposed that the sole purpose of being human is to realize this cosmic consciousness. While tracing the etymology of the word *soul*, Jung learned that its root comes from the Greek *aiolos,* meaning mobile and iridescent. Jung concluded that the soul is a "moving force that is a life-force."[3]

More recently, Larry Dossey, in his book, *Recovering the Soul*, writes that the soul is an aspect "of the psyche that is not subject to the limitation of space and time, and . . . precede[s] the birth of the body and survive[s] its death."[4] Dossey admits that his definition lacks precision, and suggests that words must be allowed a certain ambiguity in order to be effective.[5] Gary Zukav, in *The Seat of the Soul*, has a similar conception of soul. According to Zukav, "Your soul is that part of you that is immortal ... [which] exists outside of time, [and] after an incarnation ... returns to its immortal and timeless state. It returns once again to its natural state of compassion, clarity and boundless love."[6] This definition corresponds closely with a Buddhist conception of soul. Although Buddhism has no exact term for *soul*, Tibetan 'soul retrieval' practices refer to the soul as *la*, or one's life force. Healing *la*, or soul, returns us to compassion, clarity, and boundless love.

Borrowing from these definitions, I use the term *soul* to mean the immortal essence of all of us, that part of our consciousness that is aware of and connected to the eternal, sacred Source of all. This *soul* awareness has a powerful energy, a moving force of a higher vibration that is healing and transformative. If we imagined the Source of all as an infinite ocean, forever expanding and eternal,

---

2 James, W. *The Varieties of Religious Experience,* 1902.
3 Jung, C. G. *Modern Man in Search of a Soul,* 1933, p.181.
4 Dossey, Larry. *Recovering the Soul: A Scientific and Spiritual Search,* 1989, p. 1.
5 Ibid., p. 4.
6 Zukav, Gary. *The Seat of the Soul,* 1990, p. 30-35.

an individual soul would be a droplet of water taken from this vast ocean. This droplet resides in each and every living being. As the seed of consciousness that carries the memory of the divine, the soul desires to reunite and return to its Source, the ground of its being. Although the soul is the *essence* of our *being*, it can become fractured by fears, desires, and traumatic experiences. This is what is meant by soul loss.

The powerful impact of a crisis, though painful and frightening, can be the 'requisite stimulus' that shatters the illusions of a limited worldview, and unbinds the *divine germ* that is hidden within us. A new sense of self can emerge, one that is boundless, beyond our personal identity or ego. This Essential Self, unshackled from preconceptions and indoctrination, filled with compassionate awareness, gives us a sense of peace and equanimity. *Unbinding the Soul* shows how trauma or crisis can serve as a powerful tool to unlock the door to our awareness of our Essential Self and begin the process of healing. Having our psyches cracked open, and bringing compassionate awareness to our wounds, allows a light to shine on the darkness of our being. Unbinding our souls fills us with a new sense of purpose and radiance, allowing us to truly feel whole.

However, as anyone who has suffered knows, crisis is also a dangerous time of uncertainties. When faced with a devastating loss, whether through divorce, severe illness, death or natural catastrophe, our world is shattered, sending us into states of chaos, confusion and anxiety. We stand precariously on the razor's edge of an abyss. The purpose of this book is to provide a road map for navigating this foreign and treacherous terrain, to show us how, contrary to conventional wisdom, crisis can be transformed into blessing. Drawing from my own crisis and journey of discovery, *Unbinding the Soul* introduces an integrated model of healing. As a psychotherapist trained not to self-disclose, initially I struggled with the decision to share the details of my personal history. However, the inspiring words of Alice Walker, author of *The Color Purple*, removed my doubts and reinforced the relevance of sharing the depths of my own suffering. She says, "Story telling is itself a healing process . . . once you get [the stories], they become a fabric of your whole. That is why they heal you."[7]

In narrative theology, story telling becomes a therapeutic tool. Sharing our story revives our past, sheds light on the present, and implicates the future. Story telling allows us to learn from our past in order to heal our present predicaments.[8] However, we must distinguish between reflecting on our past with the light of awareness and simply rehashing events. Reflection illuminates and heals, while rehashing reinforces identification with our wounds. While some spiritual traditions focus on transcending the human story, I believe the way to uncovering the 'divine germ' and unbinding our souls is by diving in and closely examining our emotional wounds with light of compassionate awareness. Through developing this expanded awareness, we can see a crisis, or any challenge, in a new light and begin the long process of transformation.

THE STRUCTURE OF THE BOOK

This structure of *Unbinding the Soul* follows the Buddhist way of examining one's mind. The book is divided into three major sections: *View, Path* and *Fruition*. Part I, *The View*, refers to the ground from which our perception of reality and 'the self' arises. Depending on our view of life and our experience, we believe and react to stimuli in a particular fashion, either moving towards freedom and joy, or toward constriction and fear. Chapter One, *The Fire of Initiation,* illustrates how crisis can become a rite of passage. Crisis challenges our existing beliefs and self-identity, burnt off by our pain, ultimately revealing our primordial, true self. The chapter describes the stages of personal crisis and introduces 'the hero's journey' as a method for moving through crisis to self-transformation.

Chapter Two, *The Journey of The Self*, discusses pertinent psychological research about how our identities are a product of our emotional reactions,

---

[7] Walker, A. 1990. Interview in *Common Boundary*.
[8] See Appendix Four on Domains of Integration. Integrating our narrative is part of our development.

which are in turn connected to our biological nervous system and our environment. Chapter Three, *Shattering Illusions*, describes the chaotic physical, emotional and psychological states we experience during a crisis, highlighting how crisis shatters defenses and false beliefs, and opens us up to a deeper, more authentic Essential Self.

Part II, *The Path*, focuses on methods of meditation and awareness training that help to stabilize the mind, create a vessel to transform overwhelming emotions, and access higher states of consciousness. Like a deep-sea diver, we can only descend into the depths of awareness equipped with a special apparatus. The following chapters provide the tools needed to navigate the way through the tunnel of suffering into the light of awareness. Chapter Four, *The Radiant Heart*, explores the meaning of compassion, and the importance of cultivating this quality in ourselves and others. Developing our own compassionate observer becomes the key to bringing light into the darkness of being. Chapter Five, *Mindful Listening*, introduces the Chinese symbol for *listen* as a metaphor to facilitate silence, stillness and breath, essential tools to soothe suffering and promote clarity. Chapter Six, *Riding the Waves of Emotions*, draws from the Buddhist teachings of 'monkey mind' and how to tame our hopping, reactive thoughts and emotions. Chapter Seven, *The Heart-Mind Transformation Process*, describes a model of healing that integrates expanded awareness, compassionate wisdom, with recent researches on our brains, heart intelligence and mind-body connection.

Part III, *Fruition*, describes how to harvest and savor the fruits of our labors, how we celebrate the gift of cultivating our compassionate observer, and allowing the light of awareness to unbind our souls and heal our trauma. Chapter Eight, *The Dance of Awareness*, illustrates the process of connecting to our expanded awareness, and integrating the disowned aspects of ourselves. Chapter Nine, *Beyond Hope and Fear*, illuminates the transformation that frees us from the enslavement of our attachments and fears. We can learn to shed guilt, regret and worry, learn to live in the now, surrender to the flow of the present moment and connect to our essence. The appendices detail relevant information about Interpersonal Neurobiology, the brain and meditation.

As we begin our journey together, I would like to share these inspiring lyrics from the great poet musician, Leonard Cohen:

> Ring the bells that still can ring.
> Forget the perfect offering.
> There is a crack in everything.
> That is where the light can enter.

PART ONE
THE VIEW

CHAPTER ONE

The Fire of Initiation

There is no birth of consciousness without pain.
C.G. Jung

A hand moves, and the fire's whirling takes different shapes,
All things change when we do.
Kukai

On a Friday evening in May of 2007, the citizens of Greensburg, Kansas looked out their windows, or up from their front porch swings, and saw something magnificent. Their azure sky was filled with an amazing display of lights, a glorious and magical phenomenon of Mother Nature. The source of this display was a series of electrical storms to which the residents had long grown accustomed. So, after the show, most of the residents went to bed, thinking no more of it. Soon after, however, phones started ringing. This was an emergency. The citizens of Greensburg had thirty minutes to evacuate their homes and get to safety. Unbeknownst to them, the colorful, beautiful lights of early evening presaged an on-coming tornado, a monster with winds up to 200 miles per hour.

Among the residents who prepared for this onslaught was Dennis and his 14-year-old daughter, Lindy, who huddled together in their basement. The tornado hit like an exploding bomb, shattering all about them. Emerging from the wreckage, shaken but intact, Dennis and Lindy surveyed the devastation. Their entire community lay in ruins. Suddenly, and with little warning, Dennis, Lindy and the denizens of Greensburg had lost everything. Or had they?

What is so extraordinary about the Greensburg tragedy is the reaction of Dennis, Lindy and their fellow survivors. Instead of despair, Dennis experienced tremendous joy and gratitude. After a crisis of such magnitude, how could he feel grateful? Was he merely relieved for having survived the disaster? No, it was much more than that. During interviews with the press, Dennis acknowledged that he and his fellow residents would need to grieve for their overwhelming loss. But he added, "As we get things straightened out, I think people will see the opportunities here."[9]

In crisis, Dennis saw *opportunity*. Within a year of the tornado, the residents of Greensburg emerged with plans to rebuild their town; however, they would make Greensburg the first green community, utilizing solar power and other alternative sources of energy. This is a remarkable example of an entire community that transforms crisis into an opportunity for positive growth. To what did the people of Greensburg credit their resilient response to their crisis? The residents universally highlighted their values of hard work, self-reliance, and spiritual faith. Despite, or perhaps because of the devastating loss, their existing core values held strong, enabling them not only to cope with crisis, but also to look beyond their loss to new possibilities.

Yet another example of resilience in the face of crisis began on December 8, 2008. In a residential neighborhood of San Diego, California, an F/A- H18 Hornet fighter jet crashed into the home of Dong, Y.Y., an immigrant from South Korea. In the U.S., Dong had managed to achieve the American dream: a devoted wife, two beautiful young daughters, a promising career, and a home of his own. Dong could never have imagined, when immigrating to Southern California, that living near the Miramar air station could pose a risk. In an instant, a jet crash demolished his home and killed his entire family.

Like the residents of Greensburg, it is Dong's almost unfathomable reaction that makes his story especially compelling. Though grief-stricken at his

---

9 Boyles, D. "Blown Away? Not Quite," *National Review Online* 5/7/2007.

devastating loss, Dong did the unthinkable. He looked beyond his grief and put himself in the place of the pilot who had ejected safely minutes before the crash. In interviews with the press, Dong expressed his hope that the pilot would not suffer because of the tragedy. Forgiving the pilot for the deaths of his family seems humanely impossible. Yet Dong approached his overwhelming crisis with a deep *compassionate awareness* that extended beyond his own experience.

Do we all share Dong's capacity for compassionate awareness? Many of us would likely fall into deep despair, consumed by feelings of anger and hopelessness. The story of Karl, an affluent Los Angeles man who lost his job during the 2008 economic downturn, illustrates a dark and constricted response to crisis. Overwhelmed by despair, Karl descended into a deep and intractable depression. Unemployed for many months, and seeing no end to his suffering, Karl succumbed to his despair by ending his life. However, believing that death was 'more honorable' than poverty, Karl took the lives of wife and children as well. Lacking the expanded awareness of Dennis and Dong, Karl could only envision a future of isolation and destitution, the extreme and dark response to crisis.

At a moment of terrifying loss, some, like the residents of Greensburg and Dong, respond with hope and compassion, while others, like Karl, succumb to their despair. Humans are capable of extreme responses to crises. What makes the difference is perspective, a difference recalled in a wise Japanese parable.

Long, long ago, a samurai sought the counsel of a wise elderly monk, asking him to reveal the meaning of heaven and hell. Rather than answer the question directly, the monk turned and walked away. The samurai took the monk's response as a grave insult. With brandished sword, the warrior pursued the old monk. At the moment before the fatal blow, the monk turned, and with heartfelt compassion, looked deep into the eyes of the young warrior, gently replying, "This is hell." Instantly, the samurai understood the meaning of the monk's message. Overcome with gratitude and humility, the samurai sank to his knees, honoring the monk for the gift of awakening. The monk looked upon the humble warrior with smiling eyes and said, "This is heaven."

This fable illustrates how emotions and beliefs need not imprison us in a limited, constricted perspective of our reality. Like the samurai, we can awaken to the possibility of an alternative view. We can *choose* our responses to what life presents to us. A challenging situation, even a devastating crisis, need not become our living hell, an abyss from which there is no escape. Within each personal crisis there exists a potential for transformation and expanded awareness.

THE DEFINITION OF CRISIS

Crisis is a time of chaos and upheaval. But, as the Greensburg residents revealed, crisis can expose a juncture that leads to positive change. An enduring popular misconception exists regarding the Chinese symbol for crisis (*xei ji*). This misconception defines the character as having two parts: *danger* and *opportunity*. However, Victor Mair, a regarded Chinese historian and linguist, identifies the accurate translation as *danger* (xei) [top character], and *juncture* or *moment* (ji) [below]. The Chinese symbol for *opportunity* is a combination of the characters (ji) *juncture* or *moment* [top character], and (wei) *occasion*, which suggests a time of favor or benefit [see Illustrations below].

Danger

Juncture or Moment

Juncture or Moment

Occasion

Crisis

Opportunity

Therefore, the Chinese character for crisis does not directly imply opportunity, but a juncture or a moment that can reveal a novel outcome. Opportunity implies favor, where juncture suggests potential, which is a subtle but profound difference. The Chinese character for *danger* describes existing on the edge of a precipice, and the character for *juncture* indicates that one's decisions and actions, at a particular moment, will determine the outcome. *Crisis, then, can be either a vehicle for growth or for devastation.*

From the Western perspective, the root of the word *crisis* is derived from the Greek, *krisis* or *krinein*, meaning to *separate* and *decide*, and the Latin for *judgment*. Webster's dictionary defines crisis as "a crucial or decisive point or situation; a turning point . . . an emotionally stressful event or traumatc change in a person's life." Synthesizing the Eastern and Western perspectives, crisis can be defined as an *emotionally stressful or traumatic point in one's life, requiring decisive actions and judgments that will determine the outcome.*

Traumatic events such as natural disasters, job loss, divorce, illness or the death of a loved one can threaten our sense of security and how we define ourselves. Our responses to these events reflect how we view the world and ourselves. Crisis can either expand our perspective or shut us down, forcing us retreat to habitual and often inadequate responses. As a catalyst for change, crisis challenges our old patterns of thinking and being, patterns heavily influenced by our families, our communities, and our cultures. Some of our habitual patterns of thought and behavior undermine a positive, constructive adaptation to crisis. By unsettling the foundation of our core values and beliefs, crisis can shatter conditioned perceptions, introducing us to new ways of experiencing the world.

Although crisis can serve as a wake-up call, we must invoke the courage and capacity, to say, 'Yes!' to the journey toward healing. If our response to crisis is to panic and retreat, we will become frozen and immobilized. The feelings of shock, anger, doubt and shame can overwhelm us, obscuring our view of a possible and positive future, clouding our vision of a light at the end of the tunnel.

Complex organisms, such as humans, develop through a process of adaptation and integration. Although we are all biologically hardwired to adapt to change, we are not all equipped with the same tools. Some of us are resilient and adaptable, while others steadfastly resist changing. *Resilience* is a key aspect to embracing an expanded awareness, of considering new and novel possibilities. Through connection to our expanded awareness we are all capable of healing and transforming the suffering caused by unexpected tragedies.

Our psyches can be likened to the steel that is tempered by a master swordsmith. With an expanded awareness, a trauma can make us stronger and more flexible. Without it, the red-hot fire will burn us, leaving us charred and brittle. We can rarely predict when a crisis will come. With little control over the behaviors of others and no control over the forces of nature, life is dangerous and unpredictable. However, when faced with tragedy, we can choose how to respond.

With the gift of expanded awareness we can use crisis as a vehicle for positive change, both individually and collectively. Expanded awareness gives meaning to crisis, allowing us to view our tragedies and losses not simply as ends but as new beginnings, junctures with a potential for personal growth. Through expanded awareness we can see crisis as a form of initiation, to shed outmoded views and identities and to adopt new perspectives and insights. We can open ourselves to the *possibility* for positive change.

CRISIS AS INITIATION

In the ancient wisdom of the Ndembu, a tribal people of Southern Africa, a boy must shed his childhood identity by becoming a *mwadi*, an initiate who endures a rite of passage in order to join the adult men of his tribe.[10] The *mwadi* must leave the comfort of his mother and undergo a four-month ritual, guided by tribal elders, of circumcision, hazing and rigorous education. Although harrowing and traumatic, the Ndembu view this initiation as a sacred journey, a path that leads from childhood to adulthood, from innocence to maturity, from a restricted perspective to

---

10 Cameron, E. *Negotiating Gender: Initiation Arts of Mwadi and Mukanda*, 1995.

an expanded awareness. Following his ordeal, a *mwadi* is reintroduced to his fellow Ndembu through a joyous celebration. The boy, now a man, is reborn. Armed with new knowledge and new courage, the *mwadi* is worthy of a heightened and glorified social status. Like the steel forged in the fire, the *mwadi* emerges from the flames of his initiation tempered, more flexible, more capable of coping with pain and fear and armed with the wisdom of his Ndembu lineage.

The experience of crisis, tragedy, and loss are initiations, harrowing rites of passage that challenge us to journey from one way of experiencing the world, into another richer, deeper way of being. Crisis, as in the *mwadi's* four-month initiation, connotes a time of uncertainty or *liminality*, a transitional state of *limbo* – being neither here nor there. Without guidance and support, this liminal time can be frightening, leading to confusion and doubt. Jung described this initial phase of initiation by crisis as *the dark night of the soul*. In this darkness, like the *mwadi,* we can shed our previous identity, leaving us open and vulnerable, but ripe and ready as well. Having been laid raw, we can move to the next phase, a time when we absorb new information and insights and acquire new skills. Trusted guides and champions, like tribal elders, can help us navigate and learn to see with new eyes in the dark, minimizing our experience of anxiety and uncertainty and providing the lessons and information needed for greater understanding.

Having arisen from our *dark night* fortified and renewed, we can move to the latter phase of our initiation, the *re-integration*. Just as the *mwadi* rejoined their tribe with newfound status and respect, we too must re-integrate into our families and communities after re-emerging from a crisis. We must learn to rejoin those who have known us in our previous incarnation, declaring our new identity and sharing our new found knowledge and insights with our community and even beyond. Joseph Campbell, the mythologist made famous in Bill Moyer's series *The Power of Myth,* found this initiation process depicted repeatedly in myths and fairy tales throughout the world. Campbell called this initiation motif the *hero's journey*.

The hero's journey begins with *a call to adventure*. The protagonist is summoned by destiny to leave what is known, familiar and comfortable. Enduring an intense *shock of separation* the hero ventures forth, often disoriented and ill-equipped, into the dark and perilous void. Strange lands, dark forests, magical kingdoms fraught with 'unimaginable torments and superhuman deeds' become the hero's domain. Throughout the journey, the hero learns to overcome fears and to shed inept, outmoded ways of thinking, doing and believing. Wrong turns and extraordinary phenomena force the hero to accept assistance. Help usually comes in the nick-of-time, often in the form of magical beings like talking animals and sage wizards. The hero learns to discern the sincere helpers from those whose motives are to deceive, exploit or cause harm.

By surviving torments and trials, the hero becomes transformed. With newfound courage, deepened understanding and expanded awareness, the hero returns from whence she came, bringing to family and friends what Campbell calls the *boon* or *elixir*. She re-enters her community with the gift of wisdom that can only come through the transformative power of facing the unknown and dangerous. Back in the realm of the familiar, the hero's new mission is to share her wisdom gift, encouraging others to heed the call of their own adventure and seek transformation.

In the everyday realm, as in the world of myth and fairy tales, to *fall apart* in the face of grave danger or crisis, is not considered a weakness. The *elixir* is to break open, allowing the deepest parts of ourselves to be bathed in the light of new possibility. Nature teaches us that devastating forest fires create the heat needed for certain seeds to germinate, promoting a new cycle of growth. *We too must endure our own devastation, our own inner burning, so the seeds of new life can take root and blossom.* The true value of crisis lies not in its lessons of durability and survival, but in its being a vehicle for positive change. Crisis burns away the layers of our conventional notions of reality, exposing deeper levels of innate wisdom and taking us closer to our most authentic selves.

PART ONE THE VIEW

We may take comfort in knowing that many before us have answered the call of the hero's journey, returning with the boon of expanded awareness. Mythic, historical and everyday heroes have gifted us with tools for navigating and surviving our own journey from crisis to awakening. The following three stories provide valuable insights about how we can learn from others' experiences and make the courageous choice to follow in their footsteps.

FROM PRINCE TO BUDDHA: THE AWAKENED ONE

Siddhartha Gautama was born a prince approximately 2,500 years ago, in a province situated at the base of the Himalayan Mountains. Legend tells of Siddhartha's pregnant mother, dreaming of lotus blossoms magically appearing in the wake of her infant son's footsteps. Siddhartha was born and grew up, living as a young prince, pampered, indulged and protected. His father, the king, took extraordinary care to spare Siddhartha the discomforts and sorrows of everyday life. Whenever Siddhartha ventured beyond the palace walls, the king would order exhaustive preparations in an attempt to shield his son from the realities of everyday life: poverty, disease and death.

Throughout his early life Siddhartha experienced only beauty, love, and joy. As a young man, he garnered all one could ever want from life — position, riches, a beautiful, devoted wife, and wonderful children. Yet the prince remained unsatisfied, plagued by a deep, insistent longing to know life beyond his own experience, to discover the world beyond the palace walls. Conspiring with a manservant, Siddhartha donned the garb of a commoner, fled his royal home, and set out on his own *call to adventure*.

Without his father's customary interventions, Siddhartha experienced the life from which he was so assiduously protected. Slinking through the alleyways behind the palace confines, Siddhartha came upon beggars, decrepit beings seeking food and money. Moving on, he spotted a dissipated, bone-thin old man, writhing on a stretcher. The man's stench overwhelmed Siddhartha, who had only known the sweet scents of jasmine and sandalwood. Later, along the road, he witnessed an elderly man hobbling on crutches, followed by a funeral procession, from which came the keening of doleful mourners. By day's end Siddhartha knew the existence of suffering. Poverty, illness, aging, and death shattered Siddhartha's vision of life as comfortable and untroubled. Haunted by the images of pain and sorrow, Siddhartha found himself driven to explore the mysteries of human suffering.

Siddhartha felt certain that, despite the grief of those who loved him, he could never return to the life of a sheltered and privileged prince. Holding fast to his decision, Siddhartha wrenched himself from all that felt familiar and safe, plunging into a fringe existence of danger and uncertainty. Initially, Siddhartha sought answers to the nature of suffering through a life of deprivation. Joining a group of ascetics, he denied himself all the trappings of worldly existence. Siddhartha mortified his flesh and ate so little that his body shrunk to skin and bones and his eyes peeked out from hollowed orbs. Teetering on death, Siddhartha recalled a distant memory from childhood. He allowed himself to feel the pure joy of simply sitting under a tree in the company of his father.

In a flash of insight, Siddhartha knew that joy was a part of the answer he was seeking. And to experience joy, one's body must be nourished and strong. As if responding to this reverie, a girl approached to offer Siddhartha a steaming bowl of rice porridge. Accepting her kindness, Siddhartha knew, as keenly as he had known before, that he must withdraw from his current life. Asceticism had left him weak and exhausted and no closer to finding his hard-sought answers. Allowing himself to once again grow strong, he chose the middle path, the way that exists between the extremes of excessive luxury and isolated deprivation. In this place between opposites, Siddhartha realized that the answer to his pressing question lay within his own heart.

He sat under a Bodhi tree and pledged to remain there until the truth of human suffering was revealed. For 49 days Siddhartha sat quietly beneath the tree, immersed in nature and connected to the earth, experiencing a deep state of meditation. On the 49th day, as the morning star shone brilliantly in the dawn sky, Siddhartha was blessed with ultimate wisdom. Receiving the answers to the mysteries of life and death, serenity and sorrow, contentment and dissatisfaction, the former prince turned seeker had become enlightened. Siddhartha would henceforth be known as the Buddha, *the awakened one*.

Having received enlightenment, Siddhartha set forth on the final phase of his journey. Now as a Buddha, he would rejoin the everyday world, the hustling, bustling realm of daily existence, and bear the gifts of his awakening. The Buddha would begin the monumental task of conveying to others what he had learned on his journey of awakening. The Buddha shared his first teachings at a Deer Park, in Sarnath, in Northern India. These teachings would become known as the Four Noble Truths.

TRUTH #1: All humans, inevitably and without exception, will suffer.

TRUTH #2: Anger, attachment, and ignorance are the primary causes of suffering.

TRUTH #3: A solution exists to the problem of suffering.

TRUTH #4: The answer to the problem of suffering is to follow the path toward enlightenment.

The Buddha's message was powerful, but it did not deny or circumvent the acute pain of disappointment and loss. The key to enlightenment, he stated, lies in our response to life's hardships (see Chapter 5). In Pali, the language of Siddhartha, the term for suffering is *dukkha*, meaning a constant sense of dissatisfaction. Humans have an unquenchable desire for comfort and pleasure, a steadfast attachment to the material world with its conditioned illusion that wealth, property, comfort and control will prevent this constant sense of dissatisfaction. The Buddha taught that every human is primordially perfect and whole, and each of us has the *potential* to discover our *true nature* and the perfection and joy that exist within us.

Yet, our conditioned perception that pain must be avoided, and that life is permanent and within our control, separates us from our true nature, propelling us into a striving, clinging and stumbling cycle of *samsara*, a Sanskrit word meaning ceaseless cycle of life in pursuit of happiness. As creatures caught in samsara, we may temporarily feel satisfied and content, but ultimately the feeling is fleeting, leaving us angry, fearful and anxious. The Buddha's teachings reveal that to overcome *dukha* and *samsara* we must forgo our crazed pursuit of earthly pleasure and our desperate attempts to avoid pain. We must, instead, embrace our inevitable disappointments, losses and sorrows. Through meditation, reflection and compassion, we can move through our pains and sufferings and utilize them as teachers in our journey of awakening.

THE JOURNEY OF CARL G. JUNG

Like Siddhartha, Carl Gustav Jung endured an arduous and perilous journey to bring to light revolutionary insights concerning the human condition. As the pioneer of transpersonal psychology, Jung introduced the provocative and original concepts of the collective unconscious and archetypes to Western psychology. Yet, without his crisis of awakening, Jung may have never discovered his valuable insights. Jung spoke from experience when he stated, "There is no birth of consciousness without pain." The personal and professional rejection of his mentor, Sigmund Freud, propelled Jung into a dark night of the soul that would last five long years. Awaking from this nightmare, Jung understood that an integrated and whole person is "one who walks with God and wrestles with the Devil."

Jung was born in Switzerland in 1875, the fourth and only surviving child of a pastor and homemaker. His early years exposed him to the repercussions of dark and troubling emotions. His mother was often depressed and unavailable. He was bullied at school and developed fainting spells to defend against required school attendance. Despite this early setback, Jung became a gifted student, with keen interests in medicine and spirituality. To honor these passions, Jung pursued psychiatry. During his psychiatric residency, he became the favored pupil and disciple of Sigmund Freud. However, the gifted and spirited Jung did not adhere to some of his famous mentor's theories, especially those concerning the human unconscious. Jung considered our deep, inner thoughts and emotions to be "a redeeming power of intelligence, creativity and spiritual transcendence,"[11] contrasting sharply with Freud's claim that the human unconscious is a seething cauldron of base instincts and desires.

Following Jung's publication of his transpersonal theory of the human psyche, Freud disavowed Jung, publically rejecting and humiliating both the man and his work. Jung became a pariah where "all my friends and acquaintances dropped away. My book was declared rubbish."[12] The psychiatric community branded Jung a mystic, at that time a label worse than a quack, plunging him into an abyss of isolation and shame. For five years Jung struggled with deep depression and near psychosis, hearing voices, speaking with spirits and dreaming of rivers covered in blood. This descent into darkness and despair led Jung to his theories about the collective consciousness, concluding that the "contents of [our] psychic experiences are real, and real not only as my own personal experiences, but as collective experiences which others also have."[13]

Through his dreams and reflections, Jung sensed a particular energy to the unconscious, and attempted to discover its contents and power. Seized by his own unconscious primal urges, Jung was moved to draw mandala paintings, which reflected his inner turmoil. This outward expression of his deepest pain eventually led to his emotional healing and re-integration. The more he penetrated the most remote and previously hidden aspects of his psyche, the clearer he recognized that our unconscious mind is a divine source of wisdom and spiritual transcendence. Jung came to believe that the purpose of human existence

---

11 Cortright B. *Transpersonal Psychology*, 1997, p.2.
12 Jaffe, A. *Memories, Dreams and Reflection*. 1964 p.162.
13 Jung, C.G. *Collected Works*, 1965, p.194.

is to "transform the original base nature of man into its spiritual potentiality, which it would find [in] its union with the divine."[14]

Years later, when asked whether or not he believed in God, Jung confidently replied, "I could not say believe. I know!" Without his personal and professional ostracism and subsequent emotional turmoil, Jung would not have awakened to his revelation that we hold within our unconscious a portal to transcendence. He would not have discovered the boon that many believe returned the *soul* to the field of psychology. In his final years, Jung summarized his viewpoint.

> Every problem brings the possibility of a widening of consciousness. The meaning and design of a problem seem not to lie on its solution, but in the working at it incessantly. To penetrate the darkness we must summon all the powers of enlightenment that consciousness can offer.[15]

Like Siddhartha, Jung discovered that we are born to awaken, to bring what is unconscious into the light. Our pain offers us the possibility of seeking the 'divine germ' that is hidden in all of us.

JOHN'S AWAKENING

Like many patients seeking psychotherapy, John was unaware that his personal crisis provided a rich and meaningful opportunity for growth. Before coming to my office, John had been a successful entrepreneur, relatively happy in his life and marriage. However, over the course of a few months, his successful Silicon Valley business collapsed and his marriage fell apart. Filled with anger and resentment, John succumbed to darkness and despair. Feeling acutely betrayed by his wife who could not support him when he lost his business, depression engulfed him. The attacks of 9/11 and several natural disasters

---

14 Singer, J. *Boundaries of the Soul*, 1972, p. 338.
15 Jung, C. G. Ibid., p. 345.

reinforced his belief that life was unfair, dangerous, and beyond his control. For the first time in his life, John felt helpless, hopeless, and extremely vulnerable.

Over a course of several months, John worked with me to process his intense and unfamiliar emotional pain. As he connected his early childhood of strict discipline and his need to define himself through external and imposed views of success to his present crisis, something magical began to happen. John's heaviness slowly dissolved. He began to experience compassion towards himself and others. Through our sessions, John came to realize that even as 'a successful businessman,' he never felt truly content. As I guided him through his grief, providing him with the tools to navigate his experience, John emerged with an expanded awareness and a new connection to life.

John learned not to repress or judge his fears, anxiety, sadness and depression when they surfaced. Over time, he saw his emotional reactions as signposts for further growth. Instead of accepting the role of the victim and harboring anger and resentment, John came to forgive his wife for ending their marriage. John came to realize how his previous defense of emotional detachment and professional ambition must have caused his wife years of loneliness. He grew to understand her decision to leave their marriage and was filled with compassion for her many years of pain. With his newfound insights, John re-entered the entrepreneurial community with a vision to start a business dedicated to ecological sustainability. His capacity to forgive and his new vocational passion gave new meaning to his life. As we neared the end of our time together, John smiled, sighed, and revealed, "If I had not lost my company, my marriage and my senses, I would never have come to discover true happiness."

The path of awakening is not easy. Most of us are tempted to stop 'working at it' after the initial shock of the crisis subsides. We feel content to move on with our lives, to cover the pain, despite a lingering sense of insecurity and loss. However, those of us who can view crisis as an initiation, who can 'kindle a light in the darkness of being,' will be rewarded by the opportunity for growth and transformation.

To understand how emotional growth and transformation occurs, it helps to know how the human brain develops, how we form our beliefs and develop our identities. In the next chapters, I provide an outline of the human psyche, how it develops to help us deal with personal crises and avoid the psychological barriers to the awareness of our true nature. Though the journey to expanded awareness is often long and always challenging, it holds precious rewards. As a tool for contemplation, I ask you to consider the reflection on the following page and try to be open to the questions and give space to whatever arises.

REFLECTION

Honor yourself as an initiate.
Be patient and kind, to yourself and others.
Take a deep breath, go for a walk and gaze at the stars in the sky at night.
Nourish your body.

Know that we are all in this together.
From this place of open curiosity, ask yourself these questions:

What is my crisis initiation?
What identity and beliefs are being challenged?
What do I have to sift through?
Who are my guides and helpers?
Am I open to being helped?

CHAPTER TWO

The Journey of the Self

To perceive the world differently, we must be willing to change our belief system, let the past slip away, expand our sense of now, and dissolve the fear within our minds.
William James

To know others is to have intelligence.
To know oneself is to have insight.
To master others is to have force.
To master oneself is to have strength.
Lao-Tsu

The core principle of Taoism asserts that self-mastery is what allows direct knowing of our true nature, our perfect, whole, infinite self. Some 2,300 years after the rise of Taoism, William James, the father of modern psychology, echoed this sentiment as he spoke of the need to change our existing belief system in order to shift our perception of reality. Our capacity to continually expand our perception is central to understanding how crisis can serve as a pathway to awaken to our authentic self. First, however, we must know *how* we shape our perceptions, how we develop the values and beliefs that create and inform our worldview.

We are all born into a particular family constellation, with its own script and players. Science has shown that newborns are biologically hard-wired to connect with their primary caregivers. Our relationships, in turn, influence the development and maturation of the brain and central nervous system. Out of this biological-relational feedback loop we form our perceptions, our view of ourselves, others and our environment.[16] This cycle is ever evolving and changing, constantly influenced by our relationships, our environment and our psychological reactions.

During the formative years of childhood, as we begin to create memories and beliefs about the world, we are particularly open and vulnerable to all experiences, especially those that are emotionally heightened. Our perceptions of external events are filtered through our individual temperament and genetic programming. Traumatic events can profoundly affect our developing perceptions and personal identity. However, even those incidents that might appear innocuous can have an enduring impact on a child's well being.[17] When I was nine, I experienced events that would prove central to shaping my emotional development and my personal identity.

THE SHAPING OF THE DUTIFUL DAUGHTER

On a mid-summer's day in 1961, the thick, hot air of Hong Kong suffocated the cramped, constricted apartment dwellers, who waited impatiently for rain. I too felt that still, stultifying air in my home that day. Curled up in the corner of a large sofa in our living room, escaping into the fantasy television-land of *Father Knows Best*, I tried desperately to remain under the radar of my father, who was in the next room napping. His soothing half-sleep after several glasses of Johnnie Walker Black was all that separated me from my father's raging tantrums. Suddenly, as if on cue, my reverie was broken by his shout from the bedroom, "Come over here and walk on my back!"

---

16 Siegel, D. *The Developing Mind*, 1999.
17 Kendall, E. *In Search of Memory*, 2006.

PART ONE THE VIEW

Reluctantly, I rose from the couch and slowly walked to the bedroom door to receive his orders. "Fetch me some tea, and empty this ashtray! Then you can walk on my back." My father had trained me to dig my tiny toes and heels into his fleshy back, giving him the same pleasure he had received from the Geisha girls he hired while working in prewar Japan. Suddenly and without thinking, I heard myself say, "No, I won't." This simple declaration startled us both. There was no anger or defiance in it, only an unfamiliar recognition of my unwillingness to comply with my father's demands.

Instantly, my father flew into a rage, stomping and loudly shouting obscenities at the temerity of his docile daughter. Petrified, I was immediately reduced to tears. "Stop crying!" he shouted. "Shut up, you're annoying me!" Gasping for breath, I tried to stop, knowing that according to Chinese custom, tears bring bad luck, which washes away money and good fortune. But despite my sincerest efforts, the tears kept flowing. Upon hearing this commotion, my mother rushed into the bedroom. Immediately I hid behind her, as she began to berate my father for whatever he'd done this time. Insults were hurled back and forth between them. Almost as suddenly as the fusillade began, it ended. This was a scenario my parents had perfected through many years of practice. My mother sighed and turning toward me, said, "Apologize to your father."

Ever the dutiful daughter, I obeyed my mother's request. I swallowed my truth and continued to serve my father, bringing him tea, emptying his ashtrays and walking on his back. As a subservient Chinese female, I had been taught to be invisible and quiet. Through this first attempt at defiance, I learned that to affirm my autonomy was unacceptable and extremely dangerous. I was not beaten, nor were there other visible signs of abuse. Yet this singular event haunted me for many years to come. My brain had been firmly imprinted with the message of that traumatic afternoon in 1961.

Each time this memory surfaced, my muscles tightened, my throat closed and my eyes glazed over. I continued to experience these same physical reactions whenever someone of authority chastised me. Already a shy and anxious child, I grew more fearful of confrontation and took great pains to always avoid anger or disapproval. I scanned my environment constantly, attempting to anticipate what my parents and teachers expected of me.

Terrified of annihilation, I became a chameleon, adjusting my demeanor and behavior to please others, while discounting my own emotions, needs or preferences. 'I' did not exist, except as an extension of my family's traditional expectations. As the youngest daughter, my sole role was to serve others. These relationships shaped me into an obedient, fearful, conflict-averse young woman, with no connection to my own authentic emotions, beliefs or identity. My soul would be bound up tightly for the next three decades.

The journey back to my authentic self began when, at the age of 33, I was once again confronted with tyranny and stood up to my husband's abusive behavior. However, his time the blowback was far more drastic. My husband responded to my self-assertion by committing suicide. Unable to comprehend the horror I had seemed to *cause* by asserting myself, every previous coping strategy, emotional adaption and enduring belief broke down completely. Although initially overwhelmed by feelings of hopelessness, guilt, shame and depression, eventually I made my way back to emotional stability and wholeness. However, like the initiate and hero, my return to sanity included gifts from my time in the torment and despair. What I eventually discovered in the darkness was the existence of a wise, compassionate and infinite presence. Like the Buddha, I awakened to my true nature.

This expanded awareness extended to my physical body. I experienced the novel sensation of feeling physically lighter and more spacious. As I began to integrate and stabilize this awakening, I noticed that external stressors still triggered emotions of intense despair and left me feeling anxious and physically heavy. Unlike the past, however, these familiar patterns of fear and doubt shifted when I was able to access the compassionate presence. This dance of shifting from my fear-based beliefs to my expanded cosmic awareness became the core of my meditation practice. I felt an increased openness and receptivity in my physical body, which in turn affected my state of mind. This dance would last ten years and became my decade of transformation. Throughout this time,

I pieced together information and experiences from my childhood, arriving at a place of understanding, integration and wholeness.

I came to realize that early childhood events had shaped certain belief patterns that heightened my feelings of anxiety and unworthiness. Like Pavlov's dogs, trained to salivate at the sound of a bell, my repeated exposure to intense anger and frustration taught me that life was dangerous and that, in order to survive, I should be invisible. This belief pattern began very early, taking a firm stronghold in my psyche at age nine, following the argument with my father. My father's outrage at my first attempt to stand firmly in the light and speak my truth reinforced the belief that I must remain quiet and never confront authority. Bound by these distorted beliefs, I operated from their apparent veracity into my adult life. My husband's suicide once again reinforced their truth. Life was extremely dangerous, and if I had only remained silent and obedient, my husband would still be alive.

CELLS AND THE EVOLVING SELF

Science can now measure what I experienced during my journey of awakening. We are biologically hardwired to process information, to give meaning to experience and to evolve to an expanded state of awareness. *However, a traumatic experience drastically alters the flow of how information is processed in the brain.* This alteration can cause a collapse of existing belief systems, allowing new perceptions to emerge that give meaning to the traumatic experience. Rather than an obstacle to human development, crisis can serve as a stimulus to adaption and evolution. In order to explain how we develop our beliefs and perceptions, I turn now to scientific studies in cellular biology.

From the moment of our conception, we are tiny cells composed of different types of protein and DNA from our biological parents. The living cells share similar structures that form a complex communication system. Our cells divide and grow, forming more solid structures, which become our organs, muscles and bones. The outer layer of our cells, the ectoderm, becomes the skin and is the beginning of the nervous system. A portion of the ectoderm turns inward to first form the spinal cord, then the heart and next the brain. These organs create an intricate communication network that regulates the nervous system and is central to our emotional, cognitive and physical well being.

Contributions from the fields of energy medicine, quantum physics, biology and chemistry have demonstrated that our bodies are an intricate, complex and coherent system of information processors. A biologist, Mae Wan Ho discovered that throughout the human body exists a "dynamic, tunable, responsive, liquid crystalline medium" that continually communicates and receives information.[18] From the time of conception, fetal cells are in constant communication. Every nerve fiber is encased in a cell membrane that emits low voltage currents that respond to the voltage emissions of other cells. The membranes of skin cells interpret signals coming from the external environment. This information is then transferred through the cells of the body to the brain via chemicals known as neurotransmitters, which directly affect how we perceive external information. When we confront a potentially threatening or painful experience, our nervous system emits stress related neurotransmitters, such as cortisol, galvanizing our organ systems to fight, freeze or flee. Conversely, when we encounter a person or situation that signals comfort or safety, our cells release pleasure-inducing neurotransmitters, like oxytocin, which prime us to engage and bond.

Prenatal psychology affirms that our information processing capabilities begin in utero. Along with nutrients, a mother shares her mental and emotional states with her developing fetus. Thoughts and feelings create chemicals and electromagnetic currents that flow through a mother's blood to her unborn child, affecting fetal organ development.[19] At birth, then, our physical bodies are imprinted with our parents' genetic makeup and emotional narratives. Each cell has embedded information and ancestral blueprints influencing how we respond to the external world. However, not all the imprinted information will be activated. Environmental exposure and interactions will significantly impact

---

[18] Ho, Mae Wan, *Towards a New Ethic of Science*, 2000.
[19] Grof, S. *The Cosmic Game*, 1998.

how genetic and emotional information is expressed, a phenomenon known as epigenetics, meaning 'beyond the control of genes.'[20] My own story illustrates this process of epigenetics.

MY ANCESTRAL LINEAGE: CHINA, MONGOLIA, ENGLAND, IRELAND

Like everyone, the cells of my fetus contained the imprinted narratives from my ancestral lineages, including those of my parents. By the time I was nine years old, those imprints that included fear and anxiety had been activated, operating as the dominant reactions to my environment. However, there existed within me a unique essence, that at various times tried, unsuccessfully, to speak out. My chaotic home environment reinforced my role as a dutiful, subservient daughter, while suppressing the expression of my *Essential Authentic Self.*

Lao-Tsu said, "The journey of a thousand miles begins with the first step." I was born in 1952, in Hong Kong, to parents who had transplanted from different parts of China, as the result of World War II. My father was born in Sichuan, a province in the western part of China, famous for its hot, spicy food, perfectly matching his temper. He came from an educated family and was a student of the first graduating class of the University of Chongqing, which was founded by my grandfather, who was a highly respected philanthropist. My grandmother was a devout Buddhist. Both of my father's parents died shortly after the Communist takeover during the late 1940s. As a child, I was fascinated by a photo of my grandmother sitting up straight on her deathbed. According to family lore, people in the village lined up for days to view my grandmother's body and pay their respects. Decades later, after becoming a Buddhist myself, I learned that the ability to remain sitting after death is a sign of an accomplished meditator.

Although my grandmother became an advanced Buddhist practitioner, she was not able to apply her wisdom to her parenting with her son, as she

---
20 Lipton, B. *The Biology of Belief*, 2005.

indulged his every whim and desire. Her indulgence was so extreme that she hired an extra rickshaw to follow my father wherever he went, just in case he required her assistance. The intensity of her devotion, although filled with good intentions, helped to create a narcissistic alcoholic who was prone to rage-filled outbursts. Having never been taught to break his instinctual needs, my father developed a very short fuse, and always demanded immediate gratification. Surrounded by comfort and opportunities, my father's gifts for languages, poetry, and calligraphy were nurtured by the best teachers. As a young man, my father's family sent him to Japan to study and work, where he became a connoisseur of the finest sake and developed a hedonistic lifestyle. The onset of WWII war brought his adventures abroad to an abrupt end. Armed with an excellent education to begin afresh in Hong Kong, my father tried his hand at various businesses, but with no success. Suited more to the gifts of Dionysus than hard work, my father preferred gambling at the local racetrack, playing mahjong or dancing with the local beauties.

Unlike my self-absorbed, fun-loving father, my mother came from a family filled with fear, anxiety, and shame. The oldest of ten children, she was born in the French Quarter of Shanghai, on China's eastern shore. Her English/Irish father had arrived with the merchant marines. Born in India of missionary parents, he had chosen a life of world travel and married my Chinese grandmother despite rumors of his having another family in Britain, which was a practice not unusual in his trade. Most of my grandfather's time was spent away at sea, an arrangement that suited my grandmother, who came to loathe his tyrannical abuse. My grandfather was also the source of my mother's most painful secret, a fact I would not learn until after my own crisis of awakening many years later. Because my grandfather died before I was born, the only images I have come from family photos of a handsome but stern figure dressed in uniform, standing tall as the patriarch.

While my grandmother lived until my early adulthood, she remained an enigma to me. She had been beautiful when young, with obsidian-black hair and high cheekbones that revealed her Manchurian/Mongolian heritage. According to family legend, my grandmother's uncle was a royal guard for the last emperor of the Chin dynasty. It was purported that during battle, he carried the young emperor to safety. The family's royal status evaporated when the Chin dynasty collapsed, and my grandmother grew up displaced. This was a story that filled my young imagination.

However, by the time I knew my grandmother, she had turned heavy, fleshy and sullen, not the typical, warm affectionate grandmother depicted in storybooks. I sensed a steel-like strength within her, which I both feared and respected. I often wondered at her temerity in marrying a *gwailo* or 'foreign devil' from England. In the days of arranged marriages and foot binding, my grandmother had refused both. Instead, she started a school for destitute children, going from door to door to solicit donations. She stopped her philanthropy when she married, becoming pregnant each time my grandfather returned from sea. I wondered what happened to the spirited rebel who defied cultural expectations and became a champion for those in need.

Due to financial hardship, my mother's large family lived in a cramped three-story flat off a narrow alley in the French Quarter of Shanghai. My grandmother converted to Catholicism when my aunt miraculously recovered from a serious illness after the Carmelite Sisters prayed for her. The Church became a solace for the family, especially my mother, who had to leave school to work as a dance hostess. My mother's work became a source of family shame and stigma. Salvation arrived in the form of my educated and charming father.

My parents met on a ship en route from Shanghai to Hong Kong. Their initial encounter was brief, but fate intervened and they reunited after the war when they each returned to China for a visit. Walking out the door of the home she was visiting, my mother simply happened upon my father on the street. Their initial spark ignited into a passionate courtship and they were married in 1949. I was the third pregnancy in three years. During that brief time, my father exhausted his inheritance and drained my mother's hard-earned savings.

When I was nine years old, I learned how desperate my mother had felt when she became pregnant with me. Her story began as an innocent reminiscence, a bewitching story of a beautiful Eurasian woman escaping with her family from war-torn China to be swept off her feet by a dashing hero. My mother sighed as she recounted their romantic beginnings. "Your father was a gentleman, so kind and generous," she said. I urged her to tell me more, hoping to capture the dreamy softness of her eyes and to taste the love that was once between them. But her tone quickly turned brittle as she recounted their financial woes. "I had to borrow money to pay the hospital when you were born.... I was so unsure about having a third child." Her laments threaded into an invisible cord that pulled at my heart. "Your father failed in everything, but the only good thing he did was not let me end the pregnancy. He has only brought me shame, but you make me proud. You turned out to be such a good daughter."

As a young girl, this revelation was overwhelming. Had I been a burden to the family before my first breath? Must I redeem myself by being the good, obedient daughter who would never make waves or cause any problems? Adding to my emotional turmoil was the message that I should be grateful to my father, the villain who raged at me and broke my mother's heart. These confusing and conflicting messages played havoc with my impressionable mind. Unable to seek clarification, express my confusion, or scream out my anguish, I froze, dismissing what I heard and retreating into silence.

Many years passed before my mother revealed the rest of the story. At that time, she was pregnant and desperate and she had more than contemplated abortion; she attempted it *twice*. The unknown 'medicine' she ingested gave her an excruciating stomachache but it did not kill me. My fetus was tough and struggled to survive. After two failed attempts, my mother was going to try a third time, but my father intervened, saying, "This one wants to live." So, despite her uncertainty about being able to provide adequate shelter and security for her children, my mother consented to keeping me.

Piecing together what I learned about early human development with the details of my mother's pregnancy, I began to comprehend my own personal narrative. My mysterious childhood stomachaches, fainting spells and seemingly irrational fears of suffocation must have resulted from the poison my mother had ingested and from her intense feelings of misery and despair during her third pregnancy.

Instead of floating peacefully in my mother's womb, my embryonic cells were pumped with stress hormones released in response to my mother's highly charged negative emotional states. Stress hormones, such as cortisol, directly affect our physical and emotional well being.[21] In addition, my mother's failed attempts to abort me overloaded my developing nervous system, as I had to literally fight for my life. My sister's cellular information differed significantly from mine. Born two years before me, during a time of financial stability and marital accord, my sister was welcomed and wanted. On the other hand, I had experienced fetal trauma and was born into an environment fraught with tension and conflict. Anxious and fussy, I needed soothing and comfort, which my parents did not provide. Thus, my early childhood experiences epigenetically activated a negative cellular imprint, and my parents molded me into the dutiful, subservient daughter, for whom survival meant being invisible.

THE EVOLVING BRAIN: RELATIONSHIP, NERVOUS SYSTEM & THE BRAIN

Most of my early life was spent in a mental fog. Throughout my schooling, I felt hesitant to display my intelligence for fear of upstaging my older brother, which my mother had warned me against in the second grade. I had difficulty thinking critically. I was terrified to express my own opinions, so I spent my mental energy memorizing and regurgitating information. While in college, I dismissed my achievements and lived in constant dread that the world would find me inadequate and inferior. Finally, the horror of Gary's suicide utterly destroyed any capacity I had to cope mentally or emotionally. My brain was chemically and electromagnetically blown apart. As I slowly but tenaciously emerged from the crisis of Gary's death, I developed a conscious awareness of

---

21 Hunt, V. *An Infinite Mind*, 1996.

my transformation. Not only did I begin to view myself differently and adopt a new self-identity, but I also experienced a physical change, as if my brain had been rewired.

This conscious awareness ignited my curiosity about the connections between states of mind, the brain and the body. I embarked on a journey of discovery about human consciousness and its relationship to energy. Like a child in a shop filled with tempting sweets, I devoured the fascinating theories of Jung's archetypes, neurobiology, quantum physics, and energy psychology. The focus of my study became the brain, as I confirmed what I had experienced and intuitively understood – that humans are biologically wired to experience higher states of consciousness and come to know ourselves as spiritual beings. Research indicates that a newborn's brain becomes easily overwhelmed by stimuli from the external environment. To adequately integrate and process this sensory information, newborns require healthy, emotionally responsive relationships. Prior to the advent of infant neurobiological research, John Bowlby[22] advanced the theory of *secured attachment,* postulating that because emotional bonding is vital to well being, infants innately seek to form stable relationships with primary care givers.

Allan Schore[23] described human attachment as a *fundamental* regulation system, in which parent/caregiver-infant interactions create an energy exchange that directly influences an infant's brain, central nervous system, memory, perception and sense of self.[24] When a parent and child *tune in* to each other in a way that is healthy and nurturing, their brains release oxytocin and endorphins. These pleasure-inducing neurotransmitters create a state of calm and relaxation that supports healthy development and fosters a child's ability to learn. This energetic feedback loop also promotes the coherent organization of brain structures that mediate social and emotional functioning as the child matures.

---

22 Bowlby, J. *Attachment*, 1983.
23 Shore, A. *Affect Dysregulation and Disorders of the Self*, 1994.
24 Blakeslee, S. *The Body Has a Mind of Its Own*, 2007.

The brain, the central nervous system and the body create a coherent network that shapes our perceptions and self-identity. From birth, an infant is governed primarily by the sympathetic nervous system, which accelerates physical arousal and mediates heightened emotions, ranging from excitement and joy, to fear and anxiety.[25] At about two years old, an infant's parasympathetic system becomes operational, acting as a brake to inhibit impulses and slow arousal responses. With *secured attachment*, an infant's arousal/inhibition circuits remain regulated and balanced. With maturation, a child can learn to manage their arousal/inhibition responses in order to *self-soothe* and manage life's challenges with *resilience*.

However, not all infants are born to parents or have caregivers who possess the needed resources to establish and maintain secure relationships. Without adequate attachments, infants develop faulty arousal/inhibition responses, undermining their capacity to integrate and respond to external stimuli, hindering their ability to learn or manage emotions. Throughout their lives, when faced with challenging circumstances, they will find themselves thrown into a state of uncertainty, confusion and chaos.

Nature, however, has provided a mechanism to overcome the legacy of destructive or inadequate parent/caregiver relationships. Brain *plasticity*[26] is a phenomenon that allows neural pathways to adapt or develop in response to changes in the environment. By altering our perceptions and expanding how we view the world, we can literally rewire our arousal/inhibition circuitry. We can train our brains to respond differently to stressors and challenges.[27] Crisis often exposes our existing values and beliefs to be maladaptive and insufficient. Filled with uncertainty and fear, we are invited to either rage at the betrayal of our faulty reality, or we can open ourselves to an expanded awareness, a new perception of reality that can enhance and balance the physical and biochemical structures of our brains.

---

25 Schore, A. *Affect Regulation and the Origin of the Self*, 1994.
26 Begley, S. Ibid. 2007.
27 Ibid.

A HAND MODEL OF THE TRIUNE BRAIN

The human brain is a complex, dynamic and interconnected system composed of lower and higher structures. The triune brain, proposed by neuroscientist Paul MacLean, divides the brain into three hierarchical structures, the reptilian, the limbic and the neocortex. These structures, which sit one on top of the other, correspond to their in-utero development as well as their evolutionary history, dating back millions of years. To illustrate the triune brain, Daniel Siegel developed a hand model. You start by holding up your hand with your palm facing toward you and your fingers folded over your thumb.

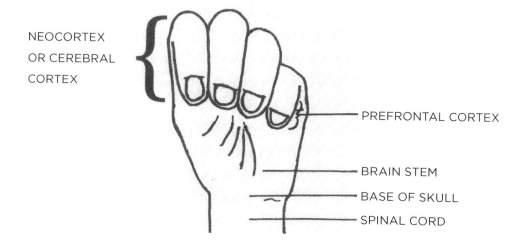

Your wrist represents the spinal cord and the fleshy part of your palm represents the brain stem. Together they represent the reptilian portion of the triune brain, which is the most basic and primal, and is responsible for maintaining and regulating vital functions such as breathing and heart rate. The tops of your knuckles extending to the tips of your fingers represent the neocortex, which manages executive functions such as language and consciousness. The prefrontal cortex, represented by your fingernails, which touches the limbic region of your thumb, is the most recent development of your brain. Only 70,000 years old, this part of the brain is now known for higher functions of integration, wholeness and well being.[28]

Your thumb across the mid palm represents the limbic region, which is the midsection present in all mammals that governs emotions and survival instincts.

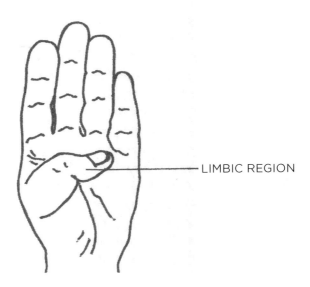
LIMBIC REGION

Positive childhood experiences are crucial for the proper development and coherent organization of each region of the brain. During crisis, when we are overwhelmed by emotions such as fear, anger or confusion, our reptilian and limbic brains become flooded with activating chemicals such as adrenalin, that send us into survival mode – the fight-flight-freeze response. If we have learned to self-soothe, to regulate our arousal/inhibition response, we can override the survival response in order to regain emotional equilibrium.

Examining Dr. Siegel's hand model, we can see what happens when we are hijacked by heightened emotions. Faced with a threat, the lower portions of our brain experience an adrenaline surge, causing us to 'flip our lids,' which is represented by our fingers extending upwards (see Illustration below). The position of our fingers, extended and separated, represents the neocortex, illustrating

---
28 See Appendix 1 for more information on the Triune Brain.

how our ability to think things through – to reason, plan and reassure – is completely sidetracked. Our thumb, the limbic emotional portion of our brain, takes over the controls and we become like chickens with our 'heads cut off.'

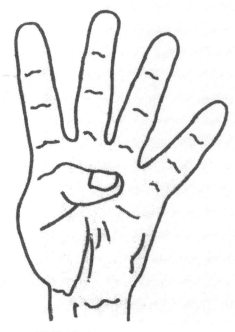

FLIPPING THE LID

MIND, BRAIN, AND RELATIONSHIP

With the basics of the brain illustrated by this hand model, we can address the question of how brain development allows us to create a sense of self. In his book, *The Developing Mind*, Daniel Siegel distills complex theories of neuroscience and developmental psychology and creates a revolutionary approach to defining the concept of *mind*. As a pioneer of Interpersonal Neurobiology (IPNB), Siegel believes that early primary relationships and the environment not only affect how our brain and central nervous system mature, but also affect how early these experiences *interact* with our neurobiology to *shape our identities*. The core principles of IPNB provide a framework for understanding the human emergence of mind.[29]

Until 1992, academia had accepted the concept of mind, but had not provided a working definition. That year, a group of forty experts from divergent fields of study, including Dr. Siegel, gathered to ponder and describe the concept of mind. Their efforts resulted in the following definition:

> Mind is an embodied and relational process that regulates the flow of energy and information within our bodies and within our relationships. It is an emergent and self-organizing process that gives rise to our mental activities.[30]

In this paradigm, *energy flow* is a process known as synaptic firing, which allows our nervous system to interpret and communicate our experience of external stimuli. *Information* is the mental representations of stimuli filtered through our perceptions, memories, values and judgments. Synaptic firing occurs when nerve cells, or neurons, release molecules, called neurotransmitters, between synapses to adjacent nerve cells. Synaptic firing is how our nervous system passes information along its vast and complex network. The human brain has over one hundred billion neurons, each having ten thousand more connections to other cells. An experience, such as reading this sentence, smelling a flower or receiving devastating news, causes neurons to fire by sending electrical impulses along their length, called the axons. Repeated experiences strengthen the connections between neurons, which form *neural networks* or *patterns*. This phenomenon is illustrated by Hebb's axiom: *what fires together and survives together, is wired together.*

The flow of energy and information depends on where and what we focus our attention. When we focus on a person, experience or memory that arouses anxiety, our nervous system will fire the neurons that signal fear. Through

---

29 See Appendix II for more information on principles of IPNB.
30 Siegel, D. *Mindful Brain*, 2004.

repeated activation by negative stimuli the 'fear' networks will strengthen and grow, firing automatically at the least provocation. *Our neural wiring influences our evolving belief system – our perceptions, values, and how we define our place in the world.* Thoughts and emotions – our states of mind – created through consistent, ongoing exposures to environmental stimuli, directly influence the neural patterns, the hardwiring of our brain and central nervous system. Because we assign more value to heightened emotions, they are encoded more deeply in our neural network and become stored as memory. *What we remember and how we feel about ourselves and the experience reinforces existing neural patterns, forming a cycle of emotions and synaptic firing that create mental models that, in turn, influence our perceptions, values and self-identity.*

Memories and emotions also prime us to scan our environment for similar experiences, causing us to avoid those that pose a threat, or to seek experiences that provide pleasure or security. This avoidance/grasping pattern establishes neural networks that form states of mind and habitual patterns, which include emotional reactions and behaviors.[31]

Even when the environment presents contrary information, indicating a threat no longer exits or that something desirable is actually destructive, we will dismiss that information, as it does not support our expectation and existing constructs. Neurons that would signal the alternative reality will not fire, thus inhibiting the *integration* of a counter-emotion or memory. Fortunately, there is a way to escape the trap of our hardwired perceptions and automatic emotional and behavioral responses. *Through observing and monitoring our automatic responses, we can modify our neural pathways.*[32]

During crisis, our expectations of reality are challenged. We come up against information that forces us to accept an alternative view. Our automatic neural reactions shut down, leaving our nervous system in a state of *disintegration*, along with our perceptions and beliefs, resulting in rigidity or chaos. New

---
31 This aversion/grasping pattern is central to Buddhist teachings, which is described in detail in Chapter 5.
32 Siegel, D. *The Mindful Brain*, 2004.

neural pathways must be forged to adapt to our new reality. Our brain can achieve a new state of equilibrium as we begin to understand ourselves and the world in a new way. A healthy brain, in Siegel's view, is always moving towards *integration*, towards improving and stabilizing the connections between its different anatomical locations and their specialized functions.[33] When the particular areas of our brain operate as a unified system, what emerges is an integrated state of mind. Our thinking, then, becomes flexible, adaptive, coherent, energized, and stable (FACES).

My journey illustrates how early childhood experiences, including those in utero, interact with the triune brain and central nervous system. As you read my story, I would ask that you become aware of how your own story has shaped your perceptions and beliefs. Which situations have caused you to 'flip your lid'? We can only change what we acknowledge. Once we are aware of our habitual patterns, we can begin the task of *monitoring* and *modifying* our reactive neural pathways.

MY UNFOLDING JOURNEY

At birth, I was filled with anxiety, creating reactive neural patterns that signaled fear and a nervous system that required soothing and regulation. I did not have a secure attachment to my father, who was seldom home, and, given his narcissistic personality, was unlikely to bond and attune to a child. Despite his emotional distance, he insisted on choosing my name, Barbara, after his favorite actress, Barbara Stanwyck. Names have meaning and resonance. The name Barbara never resonated with me, nor did my Chinese name, Lee Ching-Fan. In the Chinese tradition, the middle character is the same for each generation. Hence my siblings and my cousins were all named Ching, meaning *upright*. Chinese can trace their lineage through their middle name, which is recorded in the books of ancestors. My given name was Fan, which is the Chinese symbol

---

33 Siegel, D. 2007. There are nine domains of integration: consciousness, vertical, bi-lateral, memory, narrative, state, interpersonal, temporal, and transpirational. For more details, see Appendix II.

for *lightness* or *fragrant flower*. However, my family called me Mei-Mei, *the last one*, the youngest child.

I grew up in Happy Valley, a residential section of Hong Kong, famous for its beautiful horse race track and tranquil setting. But none of this tranquility extended to our household. At the time of my birth, my mother was highly anxious and overwhelmed by financial and marital woes. Her emotional state hindered her from developing a secure bond with me. Fortunately, I was blessed with a nanny. In the years following the war, refugees flooded into Hong Kong, taking low wage jobs as servants, and my parents were able to hire a cook and two nannies. My nanny, or *amah*, was Toh Ma, an illiterate peasant woman from southern China, who kept me in a cloth sling throughout the day and sung me to sleep with her Chinese lullabies at night. During the hot summer evenings, she would fan me while gently stroking my arm. Whenever I required comfort and security, I would go to Toh Ma and climb up into her lap. My mother, on the other hand, I could only adore from afar.

In my innocence, my mother appeared as if a queen, beautiful with ivory porcelain skin, but cool, distant and unapproachable. I yearned to run my fingers down her cheeks to feel their softness, but my mother maintained a physical and emotional distance from her children that precluded such intimacy. This lack of intimacy, however, was ameliorated by Toh Ma, my surrogate mother, with whom I felt safe and loved. Due to my in utero trauma and ongoing anxiety, I often suffered stomachaches, which resulted in crying and fussing. Toh Ma was always there with a remedy to ease my ailments. She firmly instructed me not to cry in front of my parents, for as every schoolgirl knows, crying brings bad luck. She also taught me to respect and obey my elders. I absorbed Toh Ma's love and embraced her traditional Chinese values of endurance and subservience. Although Toh Ma gave me love and security, she did not know how to help me give voice to my tears, and so I learned to dismiss the fears and insecurities that caused them.

A neurobiologist would conclude that I lacked a caregiver who could help me to name and identify my emotions, and engage my higher cortical functions. I experienced life with my 'lid continually flipped,' ready to freeze or flee from any conflict or disturbance. Given my highly reactive nervous system, I became extremely shy, hiding behind my mother, or retreating to the safety of Toh Ma when family friends came to visit. During one social gathering, I overheard one of my aunties declare that I had not inherited my mother's beauty, and nicknamed me 'the ugly duckling.' I felt shocked to hear my parents' laughter at this cruel joke. My reactive emotional brain absorbed this negative thought, which made its way into my memory and became an integral aspect of my self-identity.

My environmental/emotional feedback loop became established. The more anxious and sensitive I became, the more hesitantly I approached life, focusing on those experiences that fed my anxiety and sensitivity. In turn, this created a recursive interaction, increasing others' impatience and annoyance with me, as they tuned into my anxious energy. Even Toh Ma became frustrated with my constant need for reassurance. To avoid this continual negative feedback, I retreated into a fantasy world and attempted to perfect the role of the dutiful daughter. By the time I was five, my relationships and environment had shaped the neural pathways that made me feel inadequate, unlovable, and completely unworthy.

Although I longed to spend time with my mother, I was too afraid to seek out her company. I was overjoyed on those infrequent occasions when she did include me in an outing. It was special when my mother, dressed in her elegant *cheongsam*, the traditional Chinese dress with the high collar, took my sister, my brother and me for afternoon teas at the famous Gloucester Lounge on Queen's Road in Hong Kong's Central District. My siblings and I learned to sit quietly in the fancy restaurant with its white tablecloths and gloved waiters, serving us Coca-Cola and delicious toast, lathered with melted butter. During some afternoons at home, my mother would play nursery rhymes on the prized gramophone, and we would all sing and march around the dining table. Those were the occasional happy moments, overshadowed by the ongoing tension between my parents.

The earliest memories of my father consisted of his angry outbursts, full of obscenities. From the moment he woke up, my father would bark orders for his tea and cigarettes. My father enjoyed the finer things in life, always sporting a hat with his tailored suit and crisp clean shirt. Terrified of his fiery temper, I only relaxed in his presence when he danced. Transformed from the explosive tyrant, my father looked dashing in his impeccable suit, executing intricate and flourishing tango steps, while gazing into my mother's eyes like an attentive lover. These recitals were the only times I saw my parents appear as a loving couple. Like all children, I wanted to love my parents. But the warmth I sought deep within myself only flickered when my father danced.

My parents fought frequently. My father's rage, fueled by alcohol, filled the household with darkness and tension. Dinner times were especially challenging, the servants then becoming the object of my father's wrath. Tirades about the lack of favorite dishes or an imagined breech of protocol were commonplace. Sensing the servants' suffering, I cringed as these nightly dramas unfolded, gulping down food and blinking away forbidden tears. My stomachaches intensified as I learned to eat quickly and silently. Dining out was even worse. After a few drinks, my father became a king without a kingdom. Sauntering up to other tables, my father would force attention onto himself, his narcissism rendering him oblivious to the strange looks and sniggering of other diners. Meanwhile, I would burn with shame, feeling as though a molten lava rock was crushing my chest.

Gladys, my sister, had a very different reaction to my father's outbursts. As the oldest of three children, she was far from docile. When Gladys was born, my parents enjoyed financially stability, with the promise of my father's success still within reach. They welcomed their first-born with excitement and joy. Gladys was always my father's favorite. Even as a young child, I sensed my sister's special power over our mercurial father.

Gladys had a temper to match my father's, and she alone among the family could confront his rage. I was too young to understand my sister's pain and terror at wielding such negative power. Seeing only her elevated status, I both feared and envied her. Unable to comprehend or speak of my highly charged jealousy, desire and anger, I rejected my feeling, suppressing them into my subconscious and feeding the shadow of my psyche. The only acceptable identity afforded me, as Mei-Mei, the last-born, was that of the sweet, compliant and obedient daughter.

During my early childhood, I felt much closer to my brother, Randolph, who like me, constantly found himself on the wrong side of my father. Where I was obedient and apologetic, however, Randolph was strong-willed and stubborn. His rows frequently ended with a beating. Witnessing these severe punishments, I stood by mute and helpless, stifling my tears. I felt confused by a culture that demanded respect toward authority but ignored the rights of children. Alice Miller, a renowned child psychoanalyst, speaks of the trauma caused by this 'forbidden suffering,' when children cannot articulate their painful, despairing experiences. When traumatic experiences and emotions are denied and silenced, they become repressed, often resulting in oppositional behavior and/or deep depression.

My first memory of feeling free from the fear and anxiety, to which I had grown so accustomed, was running down the street as a four-year-old accompanying my sister and brother to their kindergarten class. Unlike Randolph, who was a fidgety and unfocused student, I loved learning and would often sit in the kindergarten class, absorbing the lessons like a sponge. Receiving positive attention from the teachers, I began to thrive, and was officially invited to join my brother's class. However, the excitement of this invitation was squashed by my mother, who said, "It is not right you are in the same grade as your brother, who is a year older. If I let you stay, it would make him feel bad." Despite my enthusiasm and aptitude for learning, my mother arranged for me to repeat second grade. Instantly, my zeal for school and life vanished. I internalized my mother's voice that told me loudly and clearly to sacrifice my love of learning and to stifle my capacity for excellence, so that males, like my brother, would not feel ashamed or inferior. Unintentionally, my mother passed on to me what she had learned from her mother – that a woman's education and ambitions are always secondary to those of men. I suppressed my desire for academic success, no longer striving to be the first in my class. But inside, I still loved learning and yearned to be recognized and appreciated for my intelligence.

As the youngest child, conditioned to suppress my authentic self from my family and the world, I found my truth and my escape with Mother Nature. I was filled with wonder and awe exploring the nooks and crannies on the hill behind my house. On the hill, I experienced a warm, beneficent presence all around me, which cradled me with whispering messages of love that soothed my suffering.

My favorite childhood haunt was my apartment rooftop. Brimming with curiosity, I would sneak up to the roof and push a plank across to the next building, thus expanding my playground. In my solitude, I would dance and twirl, like an ancient Sufi, suffused in a magical joy that sprung from deep within. Dangling my tiny legs over the edge of the roof, I sat for hours gazing at the spacious sky and listening to the voices of the stars. Without fail, the calling of my name would jar me from my private paradise, and with a heavy heart, I would drag myself down the stairs. The confident, joyous, and carefree child that danced on the rooftop disappeared as I reentered the house. Once again, I became the silent, subservient and anxious daughter.

I was, in fact, living *two* lives, one in my home as the dutiful daughter, and another outside, a free spirit who could dance and speak with the wind and the stars. My life of carefree joy abruptly ended at age seven, when after returning from a matinee movie, my mother unceremoniously announced that Toh Ma had been dismissed. In her attempt to protect me, my mother thought it best that I did not know of Toh Ma's departure ahead of time. The searing intensity of my grief was unbearable. Fearful that my deep sadness would betray my love for Toh Ma and wound my mother, I suffered in silence, escaping into a fantasyland of television. My delight in nature and secret trips to the rooftop ceased. My heart became frozen, closed to love for many years.

Unable to bond with my father, I transferred all my survival needs to my mother, becoming her devoted confidante. Wary of another betrayal, I felt my devotion tainted with caution and ambivalence. My father's eruptions left me numb and I developed a high tolerance to inappropriate behavior. To ensure my safety, I kept one step ahead of trouble, serving my father and trying to please my anxious, hypercritical mother. My authentic self would not emerge again until I was nine, on that fateful afternoon when I stood up to my father. Primed by early conditioning, my father's rage at my feeble attempt to assert myself silenced me for decades. I was not to find my voice again until adulthood, when my husband's suicide shattered my defenses.

MY CULTURAL LINEAGE: ENDURANCE AND SELF-SACRIFICE

Together with family environment, social and cultural norms greatly affect the evolution of sense of self. My family clearly shaped my identity as the subservient daughter, expected to sacrifice her own needs for those of others. In Chinese culture, *sacrifice* is a woman's greatest accomplishment and is reinforced by the many Chinese folktales that tell of women forfeiting their very lives in order to restore honor to their families. One such story was inspired by a large rock formation on the outskirts of Hong Kong that resembles a woman carrying a child. In the tale 'The Waiting for Husband Rock,' a devoted wife fears for her husband who is away at sea during a raging storm. Carrying her young child, she vows to stand on a mountaintop to await her beloved's return. Touched by her faithfulness, the gods transformed the woman and child into a rock, so they could hold vigil for all eternity.

According to Joseph Campbell, folk stories and myths hold great sway in our personal identities. Myths are reflections of the cultures from which they spring, their purpose to guide us to a level of spiritual consciousness. Endurance and self-sacrifice are paramount themes of traditional Chinese culture, historically helping people cope with political turmoil, invasions and natural disasters. The need to sacrifice and the ability to endure hardship served as psychological tools for survival and to give meaning to tragedy. As the dutiful daughter, I readily absorbed these myths and stories into my own narrative, integrating the familial and cultural messages that I was to serve others and deny myself, all the while becoming a success, yet never more of a success than a man.

I emulated my mother's passion for service, joining a Catholic youth organization, and devoting my time to serving the community. On weekends and during summer vacations, I would volunteer at orphanages, medical clinics and schools for disadvantaged children. For me, helping others allowed me to feel connected to something larger than myself and provided a constructive diversion from my own pain. Spending time with others less fortunate than myself enabled me to deny the severity of my own traumas. Although I appeared fun loving and amiable, I felt empty inside, as though something was missing. My parents were still arguing constantly, and my father remained unemployed. Fortunately, my mother had an opportunity to start a day-care center at our house, which alleviated some of the tension caused by our financial troubles.

Given these circumstances, by early adolescence I became financially independent. With money I earned by tutoring after school, I could pay for all of my own expenses and even save towards college. Chinese culture highly values education, so pursuing my studies served as a legitimate reason to leave home. My dream was to join my sister Gladys, who was already studying in Los Angeles. One of my teachers, who knew of my family's financial woes, suggested I remain in Hong Kong to become a nurse and caregiver to my parents. Hearing this threw me into a panic, until my mother finally decided my leaving Hong Kong was for the best. I would study in the United States, the country of golden opportunities.

BECOMING THE DUTIFUL YOUNG WOMAN

In 1971, at 19 years of age, I escaped Happy Valley for the first time. However, instead of fulfilling my dream to move to sunny California, I migrated to a quiet university town in Scotland. What precipitated my change in plans was not an inner calling but the demands of a man. Two years prior, David, a 23-year-old vacationing medical student from Glasgow, had swept me off my feet. A distant relative of my best friend, David possessed the alluring distinction of being the only son of a traditional Chinese family. David came to Hong Kong on the lookout for a good Chinese girl whom he could groom to be his future wife. Regarding me as the perfect choice, David lavished me with the attention that I had craved for so many years. In return for his solicitude, I pledged him my eternal devotion. During my remaining two years of high school, I refused to date or attend dances with the local boys.

With the persistence of a young man accustomed to getting what he wanted, David convinced me to give up my dream of California and join him to study in Scotland. "That way we can be together and I can take care of you." David had presumed that we would be married upon my graduation. For me, marrying a doctor from a prominent Chinese family answered all my prayers. The promise of security and the escape from the chaos at home drove my decision to marry David. I knew nothing of true passion or love. How could I know of emotions with which I had no experience?

So, at 19, I took flight from Hong Kong, quite unprepared for what would happen en route. On a long discounted flight that stopped at every major city, I fell for the man sitting next to me. Somewhere between Bombay and Bagdad, Sean and I enjoyed the easy conversation and laughter that fueled my first stirrings of passion. Fate played a hand when the captain announced that our plane had engine trouble, requiring a diversion to Belgium. The 24-hour layover evolved into a magical romantic interlude between two strangers.

When Sean and I parted in London, I knew that David and I were over. My brush with romance provided a fleeting sense of confidence and fearlessness. Despite my honest confession, David again persuaded me to change my mind. He attributed my 'temporary insanity' to jet lag. After several days of an unrelenting barrage of 'doing the right thing to not disappoint our families,' I let go of aliveness and chose security.

The dutiful daughter became the dutiful fiancée. David chose an all-female Catholic hostel for me, two doors away from his college dormitory and a two-hour drive to my classes at Stirling University. Eager to please my future husband, I settled into the bitterly cold Scottish winter and suffered an arduous daily commute to classes. Living so near to David's lodgings, I found myself doing all of his cooking and cleaning. Still believing myself the *ugly duckling*, I accepted David's declarations that I was unattractive and acquiesced to all of his instructions of what to wear and how to behave. Even when my roommate shared her concern for what seemed like my indentured servitude, I dismissed her apprehension, certain that I knew best. How could I comprehend a different reality from the one that David had defined for me? My neurobiology and my state of mind were wired to activate feelings of anxiety and fear and to minimize exposure to conflict and confrontation. Subservience and invisibility were my most honed defenses. I perversely thought myself happy because I had found a man who pledged to care for me, even though he saw me as I saw myself – the last born, unworthy and unbeautiful.

While trapped in my romantic illusions, the happiness I felt as a student was real. My early love for learning reignited in the spacious and tranquil Scottish countryside. Excelling in social studies during high school, I decided to major in Education and History. Needing one last class to fulfill my requirements, I hesitantly accepted my advisor's suggestion to enroll in a psychology course. In China, mental illness was stigmatized and conjured my own memories from the movie, *The Snake Pit*, which, as a young child, I had watched with equal parts fascination and horror.

For the class I read *Dibs in Search of Self*, the true story about the healing of an emotionally troubled child.[34] The book awakened a fascination previously unknown to me. I knew without a doubt that I wanted to become a therapist. Reflecting on my childhood days, I could trace my interest in therapy to a time when, for an independent project, I lead an experiential discussion group about classmates' reactions to certain music and lyrics.

My academic fervor and the relief from escaping my tension-filled home overshadowed my homesickness for Hong Kong's warm climate and culinary delights. A dark cloud, however, came in the form of racial discrimination when

---

34 Axline, Virginia. *Dibs In Search of Self*, 1964.

young children, unaccustomed to seeing an Asian, circled around me, made funny faces and shouted demeaning slurs. Hiding my embarrassment under a smiling mask, I ignored their taunts and reminded myself of the blessings of my excellent education and the security of being the future wife of a brilliant doctor.

REFLECTION

Take a moment to journal without judging:
What is your familial lineage?
What familial, cultural or societal beliefs did you take on?
What were significant experiences that shaped you?
Write down these milestones and observe the pattern.
What is an underlying core belief about yourself and life?
What perceived danger do you avoid about life?
What do you tell yourself or do in order to feel safe?

CHAPTER THREE
Shattered Illusions

Your pain is the breaking of the shell that encloses your understanding.
Kahlil Gibran

For the moment there's trouble, but don't be distressed. Please know the riches of the earth await you. A clever monkey wants his freedom, even from a golden chain. He's longing to find his way back to his mountain cave.
Poems of Kuan Yin[35]

To awaken from suffering is a recurring theme in many spiritual traditions, whose practices help us connect to an enlightened source of wisdom and guidance. Carl Jung believed that human growth and development depend upon our ego connecting to a deep inner knowing and intelligence that exists within each of us. Christians are guided to embrace their own sacred Christ consciousness. Similarly, Buddhists learn the existence of our basic goodness or Buddha nature, which, when accepted, can transform how we view ourselves and the world. Christianity and Buddhism both use parables to teach the importance of awakening to the enlightened wisdom that lies within.

The Buddhist parable, 'The Old Woman and the Pot of Gold,' urges us to awaken from our ignorance and discover the treasure of our intrinsic goodness

---
35 Palmer, M. *Kuan Yin Chronicles*, 2009.

and wisdom that is hidden from our view. The story tells of an old woman who unknowingly had a large pot of gold that lay beneath her bed. Ignorant of her riches, she believed herself destitute and struggled daily with hunger. Her unrelenting struggle for survival often sent the old woman far from home and even farther from her faith that comfort and happiness could ever be hers. If only she could find the treasure that lay beneath her bed, the old woman would have discovered the abundance and plenty she so desired. *Buddha* is a Sanskrit word for 'the awakened one.' The Buddha awakens from his or her deluded mind, able to see the world with a new perspective. Had the old woman awakened to her pot of gold, she would have realized that her poverty was merely an illusion. This story illustrates that we have what we need, and teaches us that to release our suffering we need to first recognize the wisdom of our psyches.

Our minds are ever evolving through a process that regulates the flow of energy and information. The deluded mind considers life a ceaseless quest for survival, perpetuating the drive to seek security through activities that keep us separated from our authentic selves, such as amassing wealth, landing a coveted job or marrying the perfect person. When, despite our acquisitions, the wholeness and security we seek eludes us, we experience a deep and visceral hunger that Buddhism calls *dukkha,* the suffering caused by dissatisfaction with what we have and longing for what we do not yet possess. The pursuit of comfort and the escape from pain results in *samsara,* the endless cycle of seeking security and that which we believe will satisfy our yearning. Most often, when we attain a coveted goal, we experience a fleeting sense of accomplishment and satisfaction, only to return to a state of want, to an insidious feeling that what we have is not enough. In Buddhism, the way through this *samsara,* the cycle of suffering, is to discover the authentic self, our true nature that lies hidden within.

MY DELUDED IDENTITY

In 1973, still clinging to what felt familiar and secure, my identity remained connected to duty and subservience. Programmed since early childhood to be a target of rage, I perceived my boyfriend's demands and controlling behavior as routine and acceptable. I thought myself content because I felt safe. I might have continued in my delusion had I not discovered that my knight in shining armor had been unfaithful from the start. Waking up to David's philandering shattered my illusions of romantic bliss and security. The shock allowed my authentic voice to once again be heard. I found courage to confront him, and this time I did not flinch nor apologize as that nine year old. I was no longer fearful to be abandoned.

Leaving David behind, my remaining two years in Scotland gifted me with a brief respite of freedom. I discovered a tenacious, resourceful part of myself previously overshadowed by my deference to male authority. By the time I earned my degree in psychology, graduating with honors, I had developed confidence in my own capabilities and felt proud of my newfound independence.

While eager to take the next step on my journey, I had underestimated the power of the familial and cultural beliefs that had imprisoned me. The summer of 1975 was filled with possibilities and realization of dreams coming true, as I ventured from Scotland to Los Angeles, joining my siblings who had immigrated there. Freed from my role of the dutiful Chinese girlfriend, I felt drawn to study at Esalen, the Mecca of the human potential movement in the West. However, my sister Gladys warned me of Esalen's controversial reputation. Still fearful of what was unknown and untraditional, I instead chose to study clinical social work at the University of Southern California.

Close to the time of my transatlantic move, my mother visited Los Angeles. In her presence, I quickly assumed my role as the dutiful daughter. At her insistence, and despite my reluctance, I agreed to meet a colleague of my sister's husband. "Gary is the perfect man for you, Barbara," declared my mother. Since youth, my mother had urged my sister and I to first get an education and then find a husband. Her advice weighed heavily on my mind. Within six months of our meeting, Gary and I were married. The antithesis of my Peter Pan father, Gary was financially stable, responsible, and quiet. Tall, handsome and very intelligent, he did indeed appear to be 'the perfect man.' A veritable Rock of

Gibraltar, Gary enveloped me in a blanket of safety and security. At that time, I felt that security meant love. Passion, with its fiery unpredictability and aliveness, made me feel frightened and out of control.

Although I had studied psychology and early childhood development, I knew nothing about how to look within my own heart. Still tethered to the familial and cultural values of my childhood and governed by my emotional brain that sought security and shrank from conflict, I unconsciously scanned potential mates to avoid gamblers, alcoholics, or womanizers. Gary was none of these. He liked to stay at home with his books and his wonderful classical music. My emotional radar was not trained to detect the danger of his dark moods or his sarcastic and demeaning remarks, which seemed tame in comparison to my father's explosive rages. I took the plunge into marriage, falling under the spell of my fears.

The marriage provided an escape for both of us. Quiet and conservative, Gary searched for a nurturing wife who would be unfailingly supportive and always put his needs first. I later learned that when we met, Gary was rebounding from a broken engagement in which he had felt betrayed by his fiancée. In addition, Gary had an ex-wife, his high school sweetheart, who had divorced him without warning. Despite his nonchalance when recounting his painful past, my heart bled for Gary. I yearned to be the loving wife who would never hurt him. From the deep wounding of our pasts, we found security in each other.

Lacking confidence and a connection with our Essential Selves, we were perfectly matched, reacting to each other from our deepest fears and unconscious expectations. Five months into our marriage, Gary's punitive, controlling shadow aspect of his psyche surfaced the instant I stepped out of my role as the obedient wife. Having just completed a major exam at USC, a group of fellow students invited me out to celebrate. Without the existence of cell phones, I simply left a message for Gary with his secretary. When I arrived home, the apartment was in complete darkness. I reached for the light and heard a chilling voice ordering me to keep the apartment dark. Gary's icy tone sent shivers throughout my body. I froze in the doorway.

Gary interrogated me, grilling me about where I had been, and who I was with. In an accusatory tone, he asked whether men had been part of the group. Stunned by this bizarre behavior, I robotically replied, hearing myself promise to always ask permission before accepting an invitation and to never stay out late or 'hang out' with male friends. Gary magnanimously 'forgave' me, allowing me then to switch on the lights and cook dinner. Like the nine year old who apologized to her father, I begged for Gary's forgiveness and resumed serving his needs. From that point on, Gary repeatedly reminded me to be grateful and put his needs first. Because he paid all of our household expenses and my tuition, my internal belief that I was a burden resurfaced, preventing me from challenging or protesting Gary's stultifying demands.

Prior to completing my master's degree, IBM offered Gary the opportunity to transfer to Germany, a move that would benefit his career but would require a three-month separation due to my graduation date. Gary did not want the temporary separation. For the first time, I had a glimpse of the fearful, dependent and depressed Gary, who needed me for support. Seeing this as an opportunity, I encouraged him to accept the offer, and reassured him that I would write daily. He agreed, but on the condition that I forgo my graduation ceremony, which would have added several weeks to our separation. Of course, I consented.

Satisfied with the arrangement, Gary transferred to Germany. During the three months apart, our roles reversed. Strangely, I felt empowered in my role as the emotionally strong partner, growing closer to Gary as he shared his fears and vulnerabilities of living alone in a foreign land. My heart melted when he expressed how much he needed and loved me. This Gary was so different from the critical, controlling stateside Gary I had so intimately come to know. Ever the romantic, I imagined running into Gary's open arms, passionately kissing as we reunited at the airport.

My fantasy failed to materialize. Gary greeted me with an awkward hug and an even more awkward silence, which extended to the hour-long ride to our tiny apartment in a small village outside of Stuttgart. Sensing his tension, and not wanting to trigger an avalanche of anger, I retreated into silence. Whatever hope I had for a closer relationship with Gary vanished when we walked into an apartment filled with unopened crates. Refusing to unpack our belongings, Gary had been living out of his suitcase. Reverting to my role as the dutiful wife, I quietly began unpacking boxes.

I became the good *hausfrau*, always deferring to Gary, who had consented to my working part-time as a clinical social worker at the U.S. Army Hospital. Discovering I was pregnant, a shift seemed to occur in my robotic existence. Thrilled and excited, I expected Gary to match my elation. Instead, he became even more sullen and withdrawn. As my excitement grew at the prospect of becoming a mother, I noticed that Gary's dark moods affected me less. Before my pregnancy, I had given motherhood little thought and felt surprised by the powerful surge of positive energy and joy I experienced. I shouted with glee when I felt the baby's movement. I would invite Gary to feel the miraculous life kicking inside my belly, but he always declined, retreating further into his shell, fearful of the prospect of becoming a father.

In 1978, I gave birth to Randy, whose arrival infused me with hope and joy, igniting a wellspring of pure love. Motherhood gave meaning to my life as I experienced a strong bond and deep connection with my newborn son. I never imagined the happiness I could feel, simply bathing, playing with or singing to my baby. Gary, however, appeared awkward and uncertain around Randy. When I expressed my joy in being a mother, Gary responded with irritation and anger. Had I known about Gary's family's history of mental illness and was more aware myself, I may have understood his inability to emotionally connect with his son, or that the strong emotions stirred by fatherhood felt overwhelming and terrifying, forcing his retreat into his books and music. My ignorance of my own true nature led me to perceive Gary's anger and withdrawal as disapproval of my happiness.

The initial joy of motherhood could not compensate for the mounting tension at home. Three years later, when our daughter, Jennifer, was born, I could no longer push away the pain. Each morning, in a perpetual mental fog, I managed to take Randy to his preschool down the street. Then I stumbled home and sat in a rocking chair with my infant daughter, staring into oblivion, inevitably bursting into tears. In the afternoons, I crawled back to bed, while the children napped, dreading the time they would wake up and fearful of my agitation with them. I felt guilty that I was a burden to the family, but I did not suspect postpartum depression. I was too busy caring for Gary when he was depressed. If I showed any signs of weakness or vulnerability, he became annoyed with me. According to our unspoken agreement, I was supposed to attend to *his* needs, not he to mine.

The advent of spring and my strong survival instincts temporarily pulled me out of my depression. I began channeling my energy into exercise, becoming addicted to the euphoria one experiences from running long distances and pumping iron. Compensating for feelings of helplessness and hopelessness, I found refuge in body sculpting and building my stamina with aerobics. I even began teaching. For the first time, I felt strong and confident. My fragile ego was strengthened by the admiring and incredulous looks on men's faces when I was able to lift more weight than they did! My long hours of strenuous physical exercise paid off when I won a local bodybuilding competition. But the attendant success and admiration I earned for building muscle could not fill the leaden emptiness I still felt inside.

My daily ritual of binging and purging began one afternoon while the children were taking a nap. I found myself in front of the television set, mechanically stuffing velvety soft chocolate ice cream in my mouth. Oblivious to the sweeping view of the forest outside the window, I took refuge in the luscious, divine chocolate nectar. Inevitably, after these binges, I would be jolted back to reality by the distended fullness in my belly, the sweetness having become a poison. I dragged my numbed body to the bathroom, where I spewed out all the goodness my binging had promised me. The purging provided a chemical release, which produced a temporary sensation of lightness and a brief respite from my pain. But the heaviness inevitably returned each day, and the bulimic cycle continued unabated.

PART ONE THE VIEW

Wrought with the shame of this crazed, uncontrollable behavior, I felt riddled with anxiety about being discovered. If Gary suspected my bulimia, he would be furious. Yet, there were many times I wished to be found out, so I could stop for a moment and scream out my pain. Unable to express the forbidden rage I felt for being trapped in my nightmare of a marriage, bulimia allowed me to symbolically act out my anguish. Gary seemed sucked into a vortex of despair and disappointment about his life, which heightened his critical, punitive behavior. My situation became intolerable when I witnessed Gary spanking our young son for making noise in a restaurant or showing fear when learning new tasks, such as riding a bike.

To see Randy quivering and wiping away tears tore at my heart, a reminder of my own pain when witnessing my father punishing my brother, Randolph. And just as before, I felt immobilized, unable to protect Randy or confront Gary. I could only comfort Randy after the fact, reassuring him that he was not to blame for his father's rage. Frightened and unable to speak the unspeakable, I continued to live in stealth-like silence, avoiding Gary as much as possible. I found refuge in motherhood, exercise and binging. My mind was still governed by the role of the subservient daughter who had no inalienable rights.

For two years I lived in denial, terror, and shame. Then IBM reassigned Gary to Los Angeles, a move that heralded a change I desperately needed. My siblings lived there, and my mother had recently emigrated to Los Angeles from Hong Kong, leaving my father to his life of heavy gambling, excessive drinking, and unrepentant womanizing. To a good Catholic like my mother, a long-distance marriage was a socially acceptable form of 'divorce.' Supported by the nearness of my family, my bout with bulimia stopped as suddenly as it had begun. Feeling confident, I began to assert my needs and told Gary of my desire to return to work. After meeting his stipulations, which included finding and paying for childcare, and making sure I would be home to cook dinner, I began working as a clinician at a nearby day treatment center for children.

As I rediscovered my passion as a therapist, I became mentally and emotionally stronger. Conversely, Gary started to disintegrate, becoming increasingly paranoid. Neither of us suspected that Gary's already fragile state of mind might have become even more vulnerable following the news he received a month earlier about his cousin, who became psychotic and went on a killing spree at a fast food restaurant. Typically quiet and withdrawn, Gary did not express any emotion regarding the incident and rejected my questions of concern. Because I remained unaware of Gary's family history of depression and suicide, I did not register how acutely Gary had been affected by the shooting. Eager to avoid confrontation, I made no mention of the incident in our limited conversations, and instead focused on the immediate task of looking for work and child-care.

I was unprepared for Gary's bizarre behavior. He began showing up at my workplace and meetings at other clinics, claiming he just happened to be in the area. One afternoon during my drive home, I caught a glimpse of Gary's car following me. Wanting to avoid confrontation, I remained silent, hoping against hope that it was just my imagination. But I could only deny the pattern of his disturbing behavior for so long. One evening, Gary raged at me, accusing me of adultery and threatening to throw me out of the house. He lunged at me, knocking me down and pinning me to the ground. Stunned by this sudden attack, I felt unable to yell or fight back. I shut my eyes, waiting for the blows.

"Did you think I was stupid enough to hit you, so you could call the police?" he said in response to my cringing. Then, laughing eerily, he got up with my checkbook in his hands. Having learned to tolerate abuse and remain silent, I did not even think about telling my family about this incident. Not knowing what to do, I did nothing. A few days later, Gary returned my wallet and apologized for his irrational behavior. Relieved that he was 'nice' again, I quickly forgave him, hoping that this was a sign that things would change for the better. But his outbursts resurfaced without warning, and each time I would retreat into silence, as my psychological shield, the only way that I knew to survive.

One evening, I heard the sound of moaning from the garage. When I went out to look, I found Gary sprawled out on the cement floor. He had covered the windows of his car with duct tape and a vacuum hose lay in his right hand. "I couldn't go through with it," he said, looking up at me and whimpering like a frightened child. "Please help me." His plea instantly melted my heart and I jumped to his rescue, taking him to a psychiatric hospital where he was admitted for two weeks. At the time, I felt relief, naïvely thinking this would end his crazy behavior. Once released and home, Gary's anger resurfaced, and he accused me of putting him into an 'asylum.' He also blamed me for his disappointing life, including his six years in Germany, which he thought had derailed his career.

His strange behavior escalated, and he began to stay up late 'patrolling' the hallways. Given the circumstances, one would think that I would have been prepared when one night he came barging into the bedroom in a terrible rage. He held a table lamp up to my face and violently shook the bed, tearing away the bedding and screaming insults at me. "You are a stupid whore!" he shouted, "And I know you are cheating on me! I am not going to let you sleep, until you tell me who he is." Gary kept shouting and grilling me about my colleagues, asking which man had accompanied me to lunch. As suddenly and inexplicably as this storm erupted, it stopped. He walked abruptly out of the room, leaving me stunned and gasping for breath.

His interrogations became a nightly ritual. The most difficult evenings were those when he threatened to throw me out of the house and keep me from the children. I resorted to sitting up at night in the children's bedrooms armed with a baseball bat, until Gary calmed down and fell asleep. Daylight brought temporary respite from the terror. During the day, Gary appeared and acted normal, as if his strange nightly outbursts never occurred. For a long time, I was too deluded and frightened to confront him. Finally the protective mother within me rallied, forcing me to act. One evening while I washed the dishes, Gary flew into a rage, screaming and threatening to throw me out. Like a soldier on a battlefield, I had become numbed and hardened, so I ignored his threats and continued cleaning the dishes.

A sweet voice broke the tension of the moment. "I am not going to let you throw my mommy out." I turned and was surprised to see four-year-old Jennifer standing between her parents, tiny arms outstretched, like a mother hen protecting her babies. She stared at her father unflinchingly, as if she knew she could stop him. Her innocence allowed her to speak the truth. Jennifer's courage stirred something deep inside me. For many years my guilt and fear crippled my ability to stand against injustice, not so with Jennifer, whose true voice liberated us. Stunned by her words, Gary ceased his tirade. Quickly accessing the abusive situation in which I had placed my children and myself, I knew I must act. The following day I faced my enduring fear of confrontation and calmly informed Gary of our separation.

Sitting opposite him at the breakfast table, I summoned the courage to speak. "I know you realize your behavior is frightening the children. Being around me only makes it worse." I paused, remaining calm but firm. "I think it's best we take time away from each other, so you can get some peace." I expected a fight, but to my surprise, Gary agreed with my declaration, offering no protest. He appeared helpless and lost. Gary had no one to turn to. I took control and arranged for him to stay temporarily at my sister's home until he felt able to manage on his own. For the next few days, before his move, Gary reverted to his quiet self, which caused me to doubt my decision to separate. I felt guilty that I was forcing Gary out of his home and away from his family.

The morning of his departure, however, Gary went into a volcanic rage, smashing furniture, breaking the children's toys, and cutting up my clothes. Jennifer reacted by wailing uncontrollably and Randy sat frozen, curled in the corner on the couch. Though shocked and stunned, I managed to grab the children so we could flee, but Gary ominously blocked the doorway. He looked straight at me and with eyes like a crazed animal, he took out a razor blade, and slit his wrists. This time, I called 911 immediately. As the sound of the siren approached the house, Gary went toward his car. Before he drove off, the medics had a chance to examine him. One of them later informed me that Gary had only surface scratches on his wrists, but because he refused treatment, they were legally bound to let him go.

After Gary drove away, I comforted the children as we sorted through their favorite toys, now broken and strewn on the floor. My heart was filled with sadness, guilt, and helplessness witnessing their immense suffering and loss. We cuddled together as I sang the same Chinese lullaby that my beloved nanny Toh Ma had used to comfort me when I was a child. For the first time in a year, we had peace and quiet. I naïvely thought the worst was over.

About a month into the separation, I was reveling in my newfound freedom with my first night out, a play and then dinner at a male colleague's home. So many years had passed since I found myself in the company of a gentle, attentive man. Delighting in the sensations of my romantic evening, I was taken aback when the phone rang. As my friend handed me the phone I had an intuitive feeling of foreboding. I froze as I heard my brother's voice on the other end of the line. "Gary is dead," he said. "He killed himself tonight." I do not remember my searing scream that I was told of later as I fell to the floor like a broken doll. Confronting Gary to initiate our separation had taken all my courage. I was finally trusting that I had made the right decision. After months of near insanity, the shock of his suicide threw me over the precipice. Suddenly, my world seemed shrouded in an eerie silence, as I remained crumpled on the floor, frozen, unable to move or speak.

With the glimmer of early morning, I stirred from my half-comatose state of shock. I had no recollection that my friend had held and rocked me, and then put me gently to bed. Dazed and shocked, I said goodbye, and somehow managed to drive to my sister's house, where I informed my children about their father's death. I will never forget how the light in Randy and Jennifer's eyes dimmed and faded altogether as they registered the news of their father's tragic suicide. Assuming my role as dutiful wife, I took charge of making all the funeral arrangements and contacting Gary's family with the sad news.

Not until I found myself alone with Gary's body at the funeral home did I finally fall apart. As I touched his cold, clammy skin and felt the sutures from the autopsy around his neck, I was overcome with nausea. I collapsed, sobbing uncontrollably under the weight of the tragedy. My mother came to stay with me and help take care of the children. I tried hard to remain stoic so as not to burden my mother, just as I had done so many years ago when Toh Ma left our household. This time, however, I could not hold back my tears. But instead of offering comfort, my mother chided me. "Stop crying," she said. "Be grateful Gary did not hurt you, too. Think of the children now and be strong." I tried to obey her wishes and wear a mask of invincibility. I wanted so desperately to march on with life. Truth be known, I was relieved when a week later, my mother decided to return to her own home.

Soon after Gary's death, I began having flashbacks and terrible nightmares. The protective shield I had erected to fend off months of terror and abuse disintegrated with the trauma of Gary's suicide. I awoke night after night, drenched in cold sweat, startled by images of Gary shaking the bed and screaming at me. In the mornings, I struggled to get out of bed, but managed through sheer force of will. I was responsible for Randy and Jennifer as well as the family income. To prepare for the separation, I had taken on two jobs, as Gary was unwilling to provide any financial support beyond what was legally required. Shaken and uncertain of the future, I returned to work after a two-week break following the traumatic suicide. Through my guilt, I never thought to ask for help, and none was offered. In the evenings, I could not escape my children's suffering, which tore at my already heavy heart. I arranged for the three of us to attend psychological counseling, separately and as a family, but the devastating horror of Gary's death kept us all in its powerful grip.

My children expressed their grief differently. Jennifer cried easily and needed my constant attention to soothe her. Randy retreated into a prickly defensive shell, which appeared impenetrable, but I sensed only thinly veiled his vulnerability and anguish. Gone was the twinkle in his eyes, the spontaneous laughter, and his enthusiastic playfulness. I missed my outgoing little boy, filled with curiosity and eagerness to explore life, smart enough to learn three languages by the time he entered preschool. In his grief, Randy morphed into a porcupine, ready to expose his quills to defend himself.

One evening I returned home from work to find Randy in the midst of a fiery outburst, his school assignments spread out all over his desk. When I tried to comfort him, he yelled, "I hate you!" His words stung, but I realized that I was the target for his unspoken rage towards his father. Randy started banging his head against the bedroom wall, screaming, "I am going to kill myself!" I rushed over, holding him close so he would not hurt himself. We fell to the ground together, as Randy continued to beat his head against my chest. I did not let go, holding him until he went limp, surrendering to the safety of my arms. Shaken by her brother's outburst, Jennifer howled hysterically in a corner of the room. Because I could not hold them both, I watched helplessly as my little girl wailed. I called out to Jennifer, trying to provide reassurance, but this did little to calm her down. By the time I had soothed and put them both to bed, I felt utterly drained, physically and emotionally. Alone at last, it was my turn to fall apart.

Soon after that incident, I had my first panic attack, which hit me while running errands in a shopping mall during my lunch break. Suddenly and without warning, my heart started pounding rapidly and my stomach became extremely queasy. My skin went cold and my palms became sweaty. I could not breathe and felt faint. Trembling, I managed to rush out of the mall, gasping for fresh air. I immediately called my psychiatrist, who informed me that what I was having a panic attack. He prescribed medication, but my inner critic judged me as weak for taking it. My mother warned me that I had to be strong for the children. Fearful of her disapproval, I hid the panic I was experiencing, pretending all was well. Inside I felt like a time bomb ready to explode. Afraid and ungrounded, I sought comfort in alcohol.

One evening, as I sat alone on my balcony, gazing at the stars that mirrored the flickering lights in the valley far below, I realized I was in a state of utter despair. I felt disgusted with myself. "It would be so easy to end this miserable life," I thought. "I am no good to anyone." This monstrous suggestion crept out of nowhere and took hold of me. Desperate to escape my demonic thoughts, I went looking for refuge in a bottle. I quickly discovered that I had forgotten to replenish my supply of wine. Wildly, I tore the kitchen apart and eventually found a bottle of cooking sherry on the back shelf of the pantry. I closed my eyes and caressed the bottle, as I emptied its fiery contents into my belly. The burning liquid seemed to smooth the sharp edges of my pain.

Then the phone rang. It was Terumichi, a good friend of mine from work. On previous occasions he had offered his help and support, which I found too difficult to accept. This call, however, came at just the right time. The sound of his loving voice penetrated my pain and vulnerability. I began to sob. I despised myself for being so weak, but the cheap liquor had unlocked my pent-up anguish, and I could not staunch the gush of tears. "It's okay to feel sorry for yourself," Terumichi said reassuringly. Despite his consoling words, guilt engulfed me as I mentally tore into myself for causing Gary's death. Terumichi listened patiently as shared my desperation and suicidal feelings.

"Nothing seems to make sense anymore," I told him. "I don't want to kill myself. There must be meaning to all this suffering." Exhausted, I surrendered to my pain, feeling completely cracked open. I wanted an answer, but the suffering made no sense. "There is a meaning to suffering," Terumichi said softly after a long silence. "Are you ready to take a leap?" His message carried a faint trace of hope and so I replied, "Yes. I'm ready to take the leap."

THE MIND THAT SHATTERS

Neurobiology reveals that from the moment of our conception, we continually scan and assimilate incoming data that informs conclusions about *the best way to adapt and survive*. As we continue to develop, information from the environment causes signals to be sent from the thalamus, located in the limbic brain, to the higher cortical regions of the neocortex. From there the signals seek to connect to neural pathways that activate our existing programmed beliefs. This thalamo-cortical sweep of incoming sensations and experiences helps to shape our state of mind, enabling us to make conclusions and take action. Our prior learning forms a lens through which all of our later experiences are filtered, thus reinforcing familiar and habitual reactions that help us survive and make sense of the world.

Identity begins to emerge from the organization of memory, perceptions, and prior learning to ensure adaptation to our changing environments. This automatic processing, which scientists refer to as 'top-down' because it requires our higher cortical functions, has great survival value in situations where we must make rapid judgments. Top-down processing can be a liability, however, when we interpret an experience as threatening when it is in fact, harmless. Without the ability to consider alternative judgments and therefore choose a different response, we become enslaved by our past, chained to a rigid, inflexible approach to life that has us react to our environment with habitual emotional and behavioral responses.

The emerging fields of neuroscience and neurotheology[36] have moved us away from Descartes' motto of human consciousness: *cogito, ergo sum* – "I think, therefore I am." Researchers have found that humans possess another level of awareness that exists beyond our everyday instinctual reactions and cognitive processes. This higher level of consciousness perceives an experience *as it is*, without bias from memory, perception and prior learning, a phenomenon Dan Siegel named *ipseity*, derived from *ipso facto*, the Latin term meaning 'as the result of a particular fact.'[37] This is what I earlier referred to as a quality of the *essential self* and *expanded awareness*. Neuroscientists have discovered that we are biologically hardwired to achieve states of *ipseity*, to experience expanded awareness and to access our essential self. To do this we must short-circuit our top-down automatic processing, strengthening our capacity to consciously consider several possible emotional and behavioral reactions to environmental stimuli. As Jung and the Buddha demonstrated, crisis can shake us up, causing us to loosen this grip of mental conditioning. Neuroscience confirms what mystics have proclaimed for centuries and upon which the founders of modern psychology based their theories – *a higher level of human consciousness does exist, allowing us to expand beyond our conditioned states of mind.*

During a crisis, our thalamocortical top-down processing becomes overwhelmed by stress-induced neurotransmitters that signal our need to fight or flee, but disrupt our ability to think clearly and respond appropriately. We are

---

36 Newberg, A. *The Metaphysical Mind*, 2013.
37 Lutz, Dunne, & Davidson. *Handbook of Consciousness*, 2007.

thrown into a state of confusion and fear. Perceiving an experience as singularly dangerous, void of value or meaning, we allow ourselves to feel victimized and overwhelmed. Our existing beliefs provide insufficient options for coping, leaving us vulnerable and uncertain of how to respond. However, neuroscientists and mystics show us that if, in the moment of crisis, we can shed our conditioned perceptions and habitual responses, then we will move into a higher state of consciousness, the place of our purest and deepest knowing. From there we can access valuable insights and information, the 'new light' that allows us to respond to trauma in a way that will help us to regain our emotional balance, develop adaptive ways of coping, and view ourselves and the world with enhanced understanding. In the words of Joseph Campbell, "At the bottom of the abyss comes the voice of salvation. At the darkest moment comes the light."

MY AWAKENED MIND

Gary's suicide threw me into a dark night of the soul. My identity as the dutiful wife and daughter was shattered and I thrashed about in a quagmire of overwhelming emotions. Nothing seemed to help. I lacked any direction or purpose. My panic attacks became more frequent, and I succumbed to self-medicating with alcohol. When Terumichi called to invite me to a meditation group, something deep within me stirred with hope, encouraging me to believe that meditation could lead me out of my madness. Yet, my Catholic conditioning created an initial reluctance, as throughout my childhood any foray into alien spiritual endeavors was considered dangerous. My mother sternly warned me against attending the group, which she decried as a form of brainwashing, readily sharing her fears that I would join a cult, shave my head, and beg for alms in airport terminals. My trust in Terumichi and my desperate need for help trumped my own hesitations and my mother's admonitions.

The meditation group met at the home of a prominent professor of comparative religion. This lent an air of respectability that assuaged my anxiety.

PART ONE THE VIEW

Feeling fragile and vulnerable in the unfamiliar setting, I clung to Terumichi like a little sister. I soon learned, however, that there was nothing to fear. As Linda, the professor and host, guided us in an open-eye meditation, her soothing voice penetrated the clamoring in my head. "Just take a deep breath," she instructed, "And gently release all the tension in your body." I began to focus my attention on Linda's face, which appeared radiant, as if surrounded by light.

Linda told us to focus on a spot above her eyes. As I followed the mediation, my body softened. Soon, tears began to roll down my cheeks like soft petals, and the heaviness in my heart began to dissolve. Linda nodded at me, inviting my grief to flow. Slowly, she shifted her gaze, although I continued staring, mesmerized by her loving energy. "Now you can close your eyes," she said, her voice guiding me into my interior world. The incessant negativity of my thoughts vanished, allowing me to listen to the faint soft music in the background and the sound of my own breath. With my inner 'vision,' I could see radiant white light cascading into the crown of my head. I felt enveloped and held in a sensation of pure *bliss*, a wholly new experience. When Linda brought the mediation to a close, directing us to 'return' to our bodies and the room, I was astonished to discover that an hour had passed. For me, space and time had become relative and irrelevant. I felt I had traveled to another dimension, one filled with healing energy and light.

I knew I had to see Linda again. Yet, the price of her private sessions fell well beyond my budget. As the gathering came to a close, Linda announced she would donate two free individual sessions. While she reached into a basket filled with business cards, which included mine, I prayed silently. On the second attempt, Linda withdrew my card. I will never forget the rapture of that moment. This was my initiation into trusting and surrendering to a powerful and mysterious higher wisdom. Little did I know the magnitude that attending the group that evening would have on my life.

Two weeks later, Terumichi accompanied me to my 'gift' session with Linda, who welcomed us warmly into her high-rise home, requesting that we remove our shoes. I followed Linda into a back room, softly illuminated by candles. She gestured for me to sit opposite her on a cushion, and once again instructed me to focus softly on a spot above her eyes. As I heard the soothing music in the background, I recognized the theme to "Somewhere in Time," a song I had been mysteriously drawn to since Gary's death.

My eyes began to feel heavy, as I struggled to keep them open and focused. Linda instructed me to allow my thoughts to flow in and out of my awareness, and to redirect my attention to the rhythm of my breath. As I endeavored to surrender my thoughts and attend to my breathing, I gradually noticed Linda's features morphing and changing, shifting from her own of middle age to those of a very old woman, and altering again to those of a young child. I recalled Terumichi's reassuring words on the drive over, urging me not to be alarmed or surprised by anything unusual that might emerge during the session.

"Just experience whatever comes," Linda said at that moment. "Don't judge what you see," she prompted, intuiting my experience. I suspended my logic and judgment, allowing whatever strange images emerged to flow through my awareness. Lights danced around Linda's body, creating an enchanting symphony of movement and shadow.

"Now you can close your eyes," her words became an invitation to deepen my journey. My body began to gently vibrate, sending tingling, caressing energy from the crown of my head to the soles of my feet. I was bathed in a warm, loving presence that penetrated the heaviness of my body. Once again, I saw rays of brilliant white light. I felt myself moving into the light, as my heart and the center of my forehead burst open. I floated out of my physical body, and as my vision adjusted, I saw a figure before me. It was Gary, his face suffused with a serenity I had never seen him possess. Our hearts opened and connected through a pulsating energy of love. I wept with joy as Gary and I communicated without words. "Yes, I am here for you and the children," he affirmed. Gary then shared lessons and wisdom from another realm, revealing the truth about reincarnation and the purpose of human suffering, concepts completely foreign to my waking mind.

"Being human is difficult," he relayed. "We fail each other constantly. The lesson is to allow love to penetrate our hurt and accept our human foibles.

PART ONE THE VIEW

You did nothing wrong. Be kind to yourself." Gary's spirit touched my tears and embraced my pain. "Slowly bring yourself back to where you are sitting," said Linda, her voice gradually floating into my awareness. The vision of Gary gently vanished. My heart felt free of the monstrous pain that had been crushing me since Gary's suicide. In its place an indescribable feeling of bliss and infinite spaciousness infused my very being, dissolving the dense, heavy sensations that had oppressed and overwhelmed me. My *soul* had been unbound and I felt light pour forth from within me. After the session, Terumichi greeted me knowingly, and said, "Something has been lifted. Light is flowing from your face." Instinctively I touched my heart. "I can still sense a warmth bathing every cell in my body, radiating everywhere, especially in my heart and forehead."

Driving home, I recalled Linda's parting words, "You might consider giving your children a gift, something tangible and comforting that can help fill the void of their loss. You've reconnected to your light. Perhaps you can share your experience with your children through a gift of love." Passing a toy store, I stopped, knowing just what was needed. Arriving home, Randy and Jennifer ran towards me. I swept them into my arms, bathing them in the radiant love I had just shared with their father. "Go and see what's in the car." Their eyes lit up as they saw two giant bears sitting side by side in the back seat. Jennifer chose the darker one. "This is my Cuddles!" she shouted gleefully. Randy grabbed the remaining bear, and held it to his face, exclaiming, "Oh Mom. It's Snuggles, and he's mine!" Holding fast to their new friends Randy and Jennifer began whirling and dancing in circles. Their laughter, absent for so long, filled the air. We began to laugh and dance together in the middle of the street.

The radiance of that blissful evening dissolved my recurring panic. For the first time since Gary's suicide, I felt alive and could sleep without alcohol or prescription drugs. My joy spread to the children who laughed more and seemed less anxious. Cuddles and Snuggles became the children's bedtime companions. Although at times I succumbed to dark nights of grief and anguish, the radiance and bliss I experienced during my evening at Linda's sustained me. I knew that Linda had more to teach me. But the cost of on-going private sessions was beyond my budget.

Six weeks after my powerful private session, I once again encountered the divine hand of higher wisdom. Although I had never bought a lottery ticket, an insistent voice in my head 'advised' me to purchase a lotto scratcher. I relented, and won $1,000, enough to cover a year's worth of monthly sessions with Linda.

A GLIPMSE OF COSMIC CONSCIOUSNESS

I felt thrilled to once again sit opposite my new teacher, whose calm, loving presence guided me into the stillness I had experienced previously. This time, however, I found myself moving through a tunnel of radiant light at great speed, emerging suddenly into a vast empty space. Floating in a blissful emptiness, I felt a powerful vibration propelling me back in time. All at once, I became part of the Big Bang, witnessing images of Earth billions of years ago. In a split second, the evolution of the universe flashed before me, from nothingness to gas, to early forms of life, to the age of the australopithecines, to the beginning of homo sapiens, to Buddha and Christ, to times of war and destruction. Scene after scene played out as one century merged into another. I observed the past become the present that morphed into a balanced and joyful future, a place of serenity and peace for all beings.

A voice emerged saying, "Humans are created to learn the ultimate lesson about the duality of life. It is your free will to choose with awareness to shape the universe. What you are conscious of affects everything. We are all one and interconnected." This voice revealed to me the purpose of our human existence. We are here to participate in the evolution of consciousness. The voice continued imparting its wisdom: "The purpose of life is to recognize the *Divine*, inherent in all beings. This recognition of universal divinity will generate compassion and wisdom, which will in turn transform human suffering and inspire service to the transformation of human consciousness. This is your work now."

Awed by this message and the presence of an indescribable love, I felt my heart blossom, opening to the pure dew of divine blessing. Many years would pass before I truly embodied this message to help others transform their suffering and awaken to the Divine within.

As the voice faded, I heard Linda calling to me from far away. Seeing myself sitting in the chair, I slowly descended back into my physical body. The sensation felt like some powerful force was heaving me into a swirling vortex. Tears streamed down my cheeks. When I could finally speak, I shared my 'journey' with Linda, who reassured me that I was not crazy. Rather, she gave my experience a name, stating that I had witnessed the phenomenon of *cosmic consciousness*. Dr. Richard Burke, a psychiatrist who wrote of his own sudden and illuminating mystical encounter, described his experience of cosmic consciousness as "a flash ... a clear conception (a vision) in outline of the meaning and drift of the universe."[38] I felt heartened and relieved to have a name for my otherworldly experience and to know that I was not alone in having witnessed a divine revelation.

For two weeks following my cosmic consciousness awakening, I remained in a state of bliss and new understanding. I began to perceive life from the mystical realm, bringing new lessons to my new roles of widow and single mother. Beneath my reactive and emotional mind there existed a calm cradling sensation, as if I were witnessed and held with deep love and compassion. "I'm beginning to look at my life with new eyes, a different way of interpreting events," I told Terumichi, a spiritual brother who understood and accepted me completely, despite all my foibles. "It's hard to describe what I'm feeling. It's as if Gary's suicide blasted open a wall separating two worlds. Suddenly, I'm seeing glimpses of another dimension."

"You're indeed waking up to a new state of consciousness, an awareness that is beyond this physical realm," Terumichi reassured me. "We hold rigidly to the beliefs that shape our reality, fuel our fears and anxieties, keeping us separate from each other and the earth. The challenges and struggles we experience break down these patterns of thought, which imprison us, keeping us on our

---

38 Burke, R. *Cosmic Consciousness*, 1962, pp. 61.

narrow path. But it also means facing our innermost fears, and going beyond our expectations, prejudices and judgments."

I stared at Terumichi, as if I was seeing him for the first time, this gentle Japanese soul with a short statue but a vast and wise presence. I chuckled, realizing I had my own personal Yoda. All at once the pieces came together. "I have been pondering the possibility that when we are in a state of crisis, or any intense experience, it could be an initiation," I said. "A breaking open of old ways of being, and opening to new modes of awareness, which kindle the Light within us."

Terumichi nodded. "It is easier if one learns to flow with the challenge, rather than to fight it or be engulfed by it," he shrugged and sighed. "It is for each of us to learn, some faster, some slower. No right, no wrong." He paused.

"This is too much to digest," I blurted out suddenly as I felt a momentary wave of both panic and certainty, having had a glimpse of the enormity of my experience and the challenges that lay ahead.

"Adopt the beginner's mind," Terumichi suggested.

"What's the beginner's mind?" I replied with a tinge of impatience and frustration.

"You'll find out. Be patient with your journey," Terumichi smiled, ignoring my defensiveness. He concluded our conversation by giving me the titles of a few books on meditation and cosmic consciousness. "One day you will teach me," he smiled, winking mischievously.

With the support of my spiritual 'team,' I embarked on the *path of awakening*. I realized that this larger sense of 'I' had always existed, but was waiting for the smaller 'me' to awaken and recognize my divine light. The crisis that was Gary's suicide shattered whatever illusions I had of reality. This shattering cracked me open to a *cosmic consciousness* and an expanded, spacious awareness which became the wings that lifted me on the journey toward unbinding my soul and healing the wounds of my psyche. The path of transformation required me to acknowledge and surrender to my pain. Navigating the treacherous terrain of suffering and confusion can be terrifying without compassionate awareness and

PART ONE THE VIEW

the other tools of transformation, which we will explore in the following section. But before we set out on the Path of Transformation, I invite you to reflect on the questions on the following page.

REFLECTION

How has a crisis made you an initiate?
Which beliefs about yourself and the world have been challenged?
Where and from whom did you learn these beliefs?
Who are you truly if you surrender these beliefs?

PART TWO
THE PATH

CHAPTER FOUR

Radiant Heart – The Healing Power of Compassion

Our task must be to free ourselves from [the] prison by widening our circle of compassion to embrace all living beings and all of nature.

Albert Einstein

Real fearlessness is the product of tenderness. It comes from letting the world tickle your heart ... You are willing to open up, without resistance or shyness, and face the world. You are willing to share your heart with others ... The challenge of warriorship is to step out of the cocoon, to step into space, by being brave and at the same time gentle.

Chögyam Trungpa

When we are in a state of crisis, we desperately need a *refuge*, a place where we feel safe and cradled. The value of refuge is illustrated by the experience of a friend, Salehe, while attending his father's funeral in Kenya. Salehe returned to his village after many years away, overcome with sadness and guilt, as he had not arrived before his father's death. Expecting censure from his extended family, Salehe received only kindness and support. The villagers honored Salehe and the sacredness of his loss by preparing a private room and taking great care to attend to all of his needs throughout his stay. Salehe spoke of the villagers' gift of time and space, "so that I could fall apart and grieve." The compassion Salehe received provided a refuge from his usual, work-a-day existence, blessing him with the physical and emotional space to heal.

Unlike Salehe, I did not have a village to support me during my time of crisis. I spent the first few months after Gary's death searching for an external sanctuary, for something or someone to cradle me in my pain and help give meaning to my suffering. I found a refuge in Linda, who guided me to my own inner refuge, to the infinite space and calm abiding I found in my encounter with cosmic consciousness. For several weeks, I remained connected to my blissful inner refuge. Then, however, the peace and calm began to subside. Desperate to reclaim my newfound peace of mind, I devoured all the books Terumichi recommended.

One evening, too exhausted to read, I sat on my balcony and gazed into the clear, sparkling night sky. As my eyes became accustomed to the dark, I saw the outlines of the mountains and trees. Suddenly, the night came alive, pulsating and vibrating with energy. At that moment, I entered what is known in Buddhism as *beginner's mind,* allowing thoughts, feelings and images to flow in and out of my awareness. Without grasping or pushing away, I was simply being present, a direct observer of experience as it is.

I began to understand the essence of a teaching story Terumichi had shared months before. The story told of a diligent and devoted student, whose eagerness to learn took him in search of a well-known and highly respected monk. After a long and arduous journey, the student found himself in the presence of the wise master. Upon hearing the student's request for teaching, the monk said nothing and simply poured water into a cup. When the cup became full, the monk kept pouring. Water overflowed onto the table. The monk continued to pour. The student gasped, thinking the master was unaware of his actions. As the water spilled onto the floor, the student could no longer disguise his agitation. In that moment, the master turned to the student and stated, "Your mind is like this cup, filled with thoughts that overflow and spill into your awareness. In order to know wisdom, you first must empty your mind."

PART TWO THE PATH

The wise master's words resonated deeply. I had been trying too hard, doggedly grasping for a desired outcome, unable to be present in the 'now.' Through my experience of the beginner's mind, I learned to honor the ebb and flow of my thoughts, without directing or pushing away what came into awareness. My fledgling ability to simply *be* with whatever entered my mind provided the space for my awakening. My old, restrictive beliefs, which valued doing, acquiring and achieving, gradually began to dissolve. In this state of calm abiding, I recalled the torment I had felt months earlier when, mired in guilt and despair, I turned to alcohol to numb my pain. My heart, which then felt bound and heavy, was now open and unburdened.

Filled with gratitude, I surrendered more deeply to this spacious sense of peace, the fruit of my meditation. During one poignant session, I began, as usual, with slow rhythmic breathing. I closed my eyes and a bright light appeared. In the center of this light emerged a soft angelic face, glowing with love. The presence began speaking to me of compassion and acceptance, and their role in transforming human suffering. "Through your pain and awakening," she said, "You will become the beacon of the Divine Feminine, to share the gift of love and compassion." As the words dissolved into silence, a light penetrated my heart and a powerful energy surged throughout my body. Awed by this revelation, I remained still and quiet, basking in her radiance. The spell lasted several hours. When it broke, I felt as if only minutes had passed.

Returning to the realm of the ordinary, doubts set in. The gravity of the message felt overwhelming. Dismissing the revelation as a product of mere imagination provided me little comfort. Fortunately, I soon had an opportunity to engage the wisdom I had been offered. One evening, while enjoying a game of marbles with the children, our fun came to a sudden and unexpected halt. Jennifer, who was losing, suddenly erupted into a fit of rage. She began yelling and screaming at me, "I hate you. I hate you!" Her eyes stared at me strangely, and she pounded the floor and sobbed uncontrollably. I made a feeble attempt to comfort her, but her distress only escalated, rendering me helpless and bewildered.

Suddenly, I felt the support of a numinous spiritual presence. Filled with a centered stillness, I sat by Jennifer in silence, witnessing her pain and cradling her in a ring of invisible light. I pulled Randy close so he could rest his head on my lap. We sat together while Jennifer continued to wail. No words were needed, only silence and my physical presence. As a compassionate witness, I sat for more than an hour, embracing Jennifer's pain and Randy's discomfort. Rather than feeling fatigued and drained by the ordeal, I felt flushed with an inner warmth, similar to the energy I experienced while gazing at the stars on my balcony. Understanding just what Jennifer needed, I carried her into the bathroom and bathed her in warm, soothing water. Her screams subsided into whimpers. Finally, she fell asleep in my arms, Randy at my side.

As I lay in bed with the children, I sensed a deep calm still radiating from my heart. Filled with humility, I began to understand the great gift of compassion, a truth so simple yet profound. By surrendering to the calming, spiritual presence, my heart was filled with light and love. I needed no words to take away Jennifer's pain. As I witnessed and cradled her suffering, the stillness and the numinous energy moving through me calmed and soothed her.

I wish that I could have always reacted with this loving awareness towards my children, but in the weeks that followed, the stress of single parenthood and full-time work weighed heavily. Exhausted and overwhelmed, I lost my connection to the spiritual presence that had bathed me in stillness and light. One night, in an attempt to reclaim my sense of peace and calm, I sat on my meditation cushion in the corner of my bedroom. I closed my eyes and yearned to again be enveloped by the healing spiritual presence. Instead of returning to a peaceful stillness, however, I was plagued by incessant thoughts. My head and my heart pounded with the wildness and velocity of a runaway horse. At the height of my frustration, the bedroom door flew open, and in came Randy. With pent-up exasperation and disappointment, I flipped my lid. I heard myself shout, "What do you want?! Can't I have some quiet time?!" With horror, I watched as tears streamed down his flushed cheeks. Filled with guilt, I immediately reached out to him. "Randy," I said, "Mommy is so sorry. I didn't mean to scream and yell at you." From under his wet lashes, Randy looked up at me, hesitated for a moment, and then fell into my arms.

Children are masters of unconditional love and forgiveness. "Mommy," said Randy, "Don't cry. It's okay." As we shed our tears together, I held Randy to my heart, gently caressing his mop of brown hair, savoring this precious moment of tenderness. Randy had grown a thick skin to protect his deep hurt. Instinctively, I began to rock him back and forth, humming the Chinese lullaby I had sung to him as a baby. We fell asleep together on the floor.

In the middle of the night, I awoke, my boy still cradled in my arms. Gently, I lifted Randy to carry him back to bed, amazed at how much he had grown. I kissed his forehead, and stood in silence, listening to his soft breathing. As I returned to my room, however, a dark energy emerged, and gave rise to a critical voice from inside my head. "How could you do this to your son, exactly like your father did to you? What kind of terrible mother are you?" These shaming words shattered the bliss I had felt just moments before. My critical inner voice held great sway. This was the voice I had been conditioned to accept and obey. Once again I spiraled into a dark abyss.

I began sobbing, feeling helpless and disgusted with myself. I felt I had failed miserably as a mother, having learned nothing at all from my meditations and my sessions with Linda. As I struggled with self-recrimination, a sudden flash of light warmed my heart, unweighting the heaviness I felt. For the first time I came to understand how harsh and self-critical I had been. Although I learned to be kind and loving to everyone else, *no one had taught me how to be loving and kind to myself.* I had created a cycle of guilt and depression, blaming myself when I 'failed' to live up to the standards exacted by my inner critic. I had not yet learned to be my own compassionate witness, how to embrace myself in the same light and stillness with which I had held Jennifer. I came to learn that to transform my own suffering, I must extend the light of love and compassion to myself, to that child who, from conception, had experienced repeated trauma and pain. I discovered that wholeness and healing do not come from extending compassion to others. *Healing must come from compassion for oneself.*

THE NATURE OF COMPASSION

The Dalai Lama teaches that compassion is an innate human quality, an elemental aspect of every being that can be cultivated and mastered regardless of religious affiliation or spiritual practice. Like the feelings of a doting mother toward her sick child, compassion is a spontaneous, nonjudgmental response to suffering, accompanied by a powerful desire to help. When opening ourselves to compassion, we must first understand that it is our desire to help that is paramount, as we often find ourselves without the resources or the power to actually end another's suffering. And, as I so acutely came to discover, compassion is not always directed outward. Compassion includes the awareness of our own pain, and a desire to help ourselves.

Two stories of the Buddha illustrate varying aspects of compassion. In the first tale we encounter the Buddha strolling through a village with an eager disciple. The two come upon an old man wearing ragged clothes and begging for food and money. When the Buddha passes the old man without stopping to help, the disciple becomes puzzled and perturbed. "Master," he asks, "I thought it our duty and our privilege to be compassionate and aid the poor." In reply, the Buddha smiled and said, "I *am* practicing compassion. Having neither food nor money to give him, I pray that his suffering be alleviated."

The second story tells of a wealthy man who sought an audience with the Buddha, asking for wisdom about how to help those less fortunate than himself. Rather than gratified, the Buddha appeared visibly saddened by the man's request. Perplexed by this unexpected reaction the man asked, "Why are you not pleased with me?" With a sigh, the Buddha replied, "Your desire to help others is good, but without helping yourself first, your wish to help will bring more harm than benefit."

These two parables provide insight into common misconceptions about compassion. The true nature of compassion lies not in finding solutions to fix suffering, but to set the intention to relieve suffering. And, as the Buddha declared in the second story, *we must first learn to heal ourselves before we can truly participate in the pain of others.*

Another important element of compassion is the notion of equality. Buddhism asserts that all beings are interconnected and interdependent, never above or below, no more nor less than another. Compassion, then, has no place for pity, which implies superiority over the one who suffers. *The realization that all beings belong to a greater whole dissolves the illusion of separation and hierarchy.* We know then that everyone suffers and that everyone has an equal right to be free of suffering. From true compassion flows proper action. We are gifted with the courage to do what is right, even when what is right is difficult, dangerous or subversive.

Finally, Buddhism teaches that compassion must always be coupled with wisdom. This is evident in the myth of the Garuda, a powerful god who possesses the body of a man and the face and wings of a bird. One wing symbolizes compassion and the other wisdom, imagery decreeing that one wing alone is not enough. *Compassion* and *wisdom* together allow us to take flight, keeping us aloft when we might otherwise feel unbalanced or exhausted. Two wings save us from drowning in our need to be helpful or being swept under by the sheer force of another's pain, resulting in burnout or compassion fatigue.

COMPASSION FOR THE SELF

Far from moving in a linear, unidirectional path, compassion is *circular*, rotating between other and self and back again. In the earlier story, the Buddha had neither food nor money to give to the old man, but he understood that through prayer and his loving presence he could participate in the old man's suffering in a way that was personal and powerful. The disciple could not fully comprehend this form of compassion because he had yet experienced its power. Had the disciple ever prayed for himself and filled his own pain with the light of compassion, he would have understood. In the second story, the wealthy man lacked self-awareness, and did not understand that before he could responsibly engage in the pain of others, he needed to look within and acknowledge his own wounding and vulnerability. My own story reveals the heightened pain that limited self-awareness can cause when seeking to help – the emotional devastation that results from attempting to fly with one wing.

Like the wealthy man, I too had erroneously believed that I should take care of other people's suffering even before I took care of my own. I told myself that because Gary was struggling, I should show him kindness and understanding, negating my own needs and feelings to minimize his burden. Also, I deluded myself that my attempts to prevent Gary from flying into a rage constituted acts of compassion. When I did commit to honoring myself, by initiating the separation, the outcome was Gary's death, causing me tremendous feelings of guilt and shame.

Because of my cultural and familial conditioning, I learned from earliest childhood to be kind, helpful and dutiful, but I received no guidance in how to assess my own needs and limitations. Unaccustomed to recognizing or acknowledging what was best for me, I did not understand that my decision to leave Gary came from a place of courage and inner wisdom, directing me to protect my children and myself. Without the knowledge that with compassion we must also apply wisdom and self-awareness, I became lost in an endless struggle of self-blame, anger, and helplessness. After Gary's death, I transferred my need to care for others directly onto my children. Ceaselessly working to meet Randy and Jennifer's needs, I continued to overextend myself, only to indulge in self-recrimination whenever I lost patience. I lacked compassion for those parts of myself that had been deeply traumatized and I would never take any time to rest.

Without compassion for the wounded parts of ourselves, we cannot heal. *Compassionate wisdom is the ultimate self-soother*, which calms the mind and spirit so we may recognize, explore and integrate that which we might otherwise reject. Recently, scientific research has shown that compassion, and particularly self-compassion, is helpful in treating feelings of depression, shame, and guilt. In Chapter Three, I discussed the importance of *affect regulation* and self-soothing in transforming our fears and anxieties. Studies suggest that training in self-compassion stimulates the brain processes for feeling loved, supported, wanted, and included.[39] When we extend compassion to ourselves – or as one of my patients stated, "When I can be

---

[39] Gilbert P. *Compassion: Conceptualizations, Research and Use in Psychotherapy*, 2005, p.253.

extra kind to myself ..." – we can acknowledge our own suffering and the suffering of others with courage, patience and understanding. I guide my patients to discover a phrase to help them develop compassion for the self, such as "I embrace all parts of me, even the part that's angry, anxious, or depressed, and with compassion, I'm learning to grow and connect to the wisdom of the heart."

THE HEART'S INTELLIGENCE

While compassion can greatly affect our emotional well being, it also has a direct impact on our physical bodies, particularly the heart. As discussed in previous chapters, all human cells are sensitive to electromagnetic fields, or EMFs. In the 1970s, biologist Bruce Lipton discovered that EMFs in human embryos are formed at the moment of conception. Embryos continually emit EMFs. These EMF's extend beyond the mother's uterus and into the physical environment where they retrieve vital information for growth and development.[40] This cellular communication system continues to operate throughout the life cycle.

The heart plays a central role in electromagnetic communication. More than simply a physical pump, the heart transmits electromagnetic energy that extends twelve to fifteen feet beyond the body.[41] Compared with the brain, the heart's energy field is *sixty times* larger and *five thousand times* more powerful, making the heart the most powerful generator of EMFs in the body. Cardiac EMF's can transmit information between people standing up to five feet apart. For this reason, we tend to feel more at ease around those who are genuinely content and calm.

In addition, the heart has its own endocrine system, producing the hormone *atrial natriuretic factor* (ANF). ANF regulates and influences our thoughts and emotions. Neuro-cardiologists have discovered that more than half of the heart's cells are neural cells, similar to those found in our brain. Thus, the heart has the capacity

---

[40] In a related discovery, scientists have found evidence for a quantum energetic communication system that is invisible to our conscious mind.

[41] www.heartmath.org

to learn, remember, and make decisions. This is why, throughout the centuries, scripture, myths, and ballads have wisely counseled humans to 'listen to your heart.'

Along with neural cells, our hearts and our brains share *glial cells*. 'Glial' comes from the Latin *glia*, which means 'glue.' Essentially, glial cells are the glue that binds neurons together. Glial cells are sensitive to EMFs, forming a powerful, interactive EMF network that allows brain waves to synchronize with the waves generated by the heart. When our heart beats in a slow rhythmic manner, the frequency of our brain waves will slow in unison. *More remarkably, one person's brain waves can synchronize with the EMFs of another person's heart.*[42]

This special interaction between the heart and the brain plays a major role in promoting physical, emotional and spiritual well being. Using spectral analysis, HeartMath researchers have discovered that the *rhythmic pattern of our heart changes with our emotional state*. Negative emotions such as anger and frustration produce an erratic, incoherent pattern, while emotions such as love and gratitude create a harmonious, smooth pattern.

Emotions affect brain waves in a similar fashion. When we feel angry or frustrated our brain emits erratic, incoherent waves, releasing a flood of stress hormones. These hormones instruct our blood vessels to constrict and our muscle fibers to contract. In contrast, when we experience love and gratitude, our brain emits smoother, more coherent waves, which release neurotransmitters that reinforce our emotional state of calm and produce a physical state of relaxation. Depending on our emotional experience, the resulting EMFs generate a corresponding heartbeat, allowing another person to directly connect with how we are feeling.

With Jennifer's sudden and unexpected meltdown over marbles, my heart synchronized with her agitation, triggering my desire to help. Initially I felt powerless and frustrated. However, my connection to spirit calmed and stilled my reactive emotions, creating an EMF with a powerful, healing vibration, a vibration strong enough to guide me to a place of clarity and Jennifer to a state of surrender.[43]

---

42 Lipton, B., Ibid.

43 HeartMath researchers named this phenomenon 'psycho-physiological coherence' and suggest that if individuals and collectives learn to promote sustained positive emotions, we can experience greater physical harmony and health, and enhance mental and emotional well being.

PART TWO THE PATH

COMPASSIONATE WISDOM IN ACTION

Practicing compassion felt easy when I opened my heart to others. Cradling my own wounds and vulnerabilities, however, felt foreign and unnatural. Yet, even self-compassion seemed remedial when compared to the feat that was opening my heart to my father. Following the separation from my mother, my father had remained in Hong Kong. I welcomed the physical and emotional distance between my father and I, especially in the wake of Gary's death. Upon hearing of my father's plans to visit Los Angeles, I knew my ability to practice compassion would be tested to the limits.

I had clung to the hope that my father had mellowed and grow wiser during our time apart, but upon his arrival in Los Angeles, I soon realized that his drinking and his belligerence had amplified. One evening, after several glasses of scotch, my father descended into his ritual of complaining and barking orders. I remained calm and disengaged. Undaunted by my restraint, he simply shifted focus, directing his verbal attack toward his grandchildren. This was too much for me. For the first time since I was nine, I stood up to my father's bullying.

"You cannot insult the children," I insisted, firing the first salvo.

"I'll say what I want," he shouted back, eyes bulging with rage. "You're my daughter and you can't tell me what to do!"

"This is my house," I retorted. "You have to respect me and the children."

"Is this the way you treat your elders?" His voice teemed with incredulity that his dutiful daughter would answer back. "You're good-for-nothing. I'm leaving."

My courage rose. "I'll help you pack your bags."

We had each drawn our swords, prepared to do battle. My adversarial reaction fueled my father's anger. He stomped around the living room, screaming obscenities, and brandishing his fists.

Suddenly, everything slowed. My fury morphed into the fierce sword of compassion, searing my anger and opening my heart. Rather than seeing my father through the eyes of an abused daughter, I connected to the suffering of a lonely old man running amok on my balcony. A surge of love flowed from my heart, holding space for my father's rage, which suddenly began to subside. Reacting with compassionate wisdom I walked toward my father, took his hands and guided him to a chair. "Sit down, Dad. You're exhausted."

He stared at me like a child. "You hurt me when you said those things," he blurted, his eyes welling with tears.

"I'm sorry you were hurt. That was not my intention." A wiser, loving, spacious voice in me emerged. We sat in silence, gazing at each other, compassion filling the surrounding space.

"Dad, why have you always treated me as a servant?" No blaming or anger accompanied my words, just a gentle curiosity for the truth. My father looked puzzled

"Why? You are my youngest daughter. You are supposed to serve me."

At that moment, all my yearnings, frustration, and pain vanished. I started to laugh. Suddenly, in a flash of understanding, I saw my father as a product of his upbringing, a man crippled by a culture that devalued women and was reared by a mother who indulged his every whim. This moment of clarity collapsed what had been an impervious wall, allowing tenderness and acceptance to move freely between us. During the rest of my father's visit, our relationship began to shift. I learned to hold space for his drunken outbursts, which diminished in frequency. Following his visit, my father remained self-centered and quick to anger, calling occasionally to demand money. Now, however, I refused his demands out of love rather than anger.

Twelve years later, I returned to Hong Kong. My father lay dying, ravaged by liver cancer and emphysema. Despite his physical deterioration, he remained tenaciously himself, boasting of his romantic conquests and hounding hospital staff for cigarettes. To avoid confrontation, my family had not spoken honestly to my father about his grave prognosis. That honor fell upon me. As I sat at the bedside and held his withering hand, I gently told him that he was dying. In this moment of intimacy, our eyes met and a deep feeling of love seemed to flow between us. My father soon fell into a peaceful sleep. I remained at his bedside, chanting the Buddhist prayers he had heard his mother recite when he was a child.

Several days later, he looked at me mournfully and whispered, "Please ask your mother to forgive me. I have not been a good husband." Tears flowed down his cheeks, which I gently wiped away. Soon after, I returned to Los Angeles. As I said good-bye, I hugged him and told him how much I loved him. He smiled and we both wept. The last memory of my father was of this precious goodbye. He died three days later.

SELF-COMPASSION – 3 EXERCISES

Learning to care for myself as I had cared for others took great effort over many months. Kindness, acceptance and forbearance became crucial antidotes to my critical self-talk, especially when I made mistakes, felt overwhelmed or lost my patience. Cultivating self-compassion was essential in honing my ability to remain patient and loving when faced with my father's anger. As the Buddha reminds us, we must first heal ourselves. When a crisis renders us helpless, invoking self-compassion can calm our thoughts and emotions, opening the doorway to transformation and healing.

FIRST EXERCISE:

The heart is a sophisticated information processing system that responds to positive energy. Bringing awareness to our heart each day is a wonderful tool for developing self-compassion.

> *First connect to your breath. Take several deep breaths. Feel your chest rise and fall as you inhale and exhale. Now focus your awareness on your heart. Ask yourself, "What is the sensation I'm experiencing? Does my heart feel heavy, tight, or closed? Or is the sensation one of lightness and peace?" If the feeling is negative, take a few deep breaths, continuing to focus on your heart. Inhale a*

color, thought or emotion that you consider positive and calming. Repeat until you restore a feeling of lightness and calm.

SECOND EXERCISE:

During the many difficult times when I found myself unable to connect to a positive emotion or sensation, rather than chastise myself, which would only intensify my negative emotions, I would practice the following exercise.

Connect to your breath. Take several deep breaths. Feel your chest rise and fall as you inhale and exhale. On an inhale recite, "Even though a part of me is depressed/angry/afraid right now, I am learning to open to love and compassion." While exhaling recite, "I release self-judgment." Change the wording to fit your experience. When you recognize and identify negative thoughts and emotions, fill your heart with kindness, patience and acceptance. Cradle your suffering in compassion to create your own inner sanctuary.

THIRD EXERCISE:

Connect to your breath. Take several deep breaths. Feel your chest rise and fall as you inhale and exhale. Feel the warmth of your breath as you inhale. Focus your awareness on the warmth of your breath flowing into your heart. Gently hold the warmth in your heart. Exhale slowly, releasing any tension. As you inhale again recite, "May I be compassionate to myself." As you exhale recite, "May I release tension/guilt/sadness/anger."

Do one of these simple *compassionate breath* exercises daily. Show yourself kindness and patience. Continue to be aware of your negative thoughts and emotions. Continue to replace negativity with self-compassion.

CHAPTER FIVE

Mindful Listening – The Wisdom of Turning Inward

To journey into this interior world within,
Love must already be awakened.
For love to awaken in us: Let Go, Let Be, Be Silent.
Be still in gentle peace, be aware of opposites.
Learn mindfulness and forgetfulness.

Saint Teresa of Avila

When you want to make a change in a situation or in your own behavior, it is essential to shift your attention from the story you are telling yourself about what is happening to the inward experience you are having.

Tenzin Wangyal Rinpoche

Saint Teresa reminds us that before we can explore our inner world of the psyche, we must first awaken to the existence of a loving presence. As noted in Chapter Four, self-compassion can be a pathway to that loving presence that cradles our suffering and brings light into our darkness. Six months after my awakening, I was learning to embrace self-compassion and to cradle my pain. For thirty minutes every night, I practiced a simple technique

Terumichi had taught me called the *heart-breath connection*. Soothing background music helped me to relax my body and focus my mind. With each inhalation, I made a silent request, "May I receive love." And as I exhaled, I prayed, "May I release fear." I added a further intention: "May others receive love, and may they release their fear." These simple yet powerful words created a calming inner refuge for my frenzied thoughts and emotions. Even during my hectic workday, I would take time to sit and practice my heart-breath connection.

With daily meditation, I noticed that my thinking became clearer and my insight more acute. I could observe my thoughts and feelings objectively and with loving-kindness. My newfound clarity gradually allowed my thoughts and emotions to arise and dissolve, like inchoate sounds from another room. One evening, while following the ebb and flow of my breath, an image came into my awareness. I recognized the image as the Chinese character for *listen* (see below). Since childhood, I had written this character many times, never considering the individual parts that created the whole. In a flash of insight, I understood that the Chinese character revealed a hidden wisdom.

Ear

Nobility

Ten/complete

Eyes

Undivided attention

Heart

PART TWO THE PATH

Listen consists of six separate parts, divided into left and right columns. At the top of the left column is the character for *ear*. Underneath is the symbol for *emperor* or *nobility*, with the top line representing *heaven*, the bottom line *earth*, and the middle line *humanity*. The ancient Chinese, as in many early cultures, considered their emperor to be the divine in human form, a heavenly emissary connecting the realms of heaven, earth and humanity. The right side of the character consists of three parts. At the top is a cross, which means *ten* or *complete*. Next is a rectangle with two lines to symbolize *the eyes of the listener*. Next is a horizontal line that signifies *undivided attention*. And the final symbol, at the bottom right, means *heart*. Carefully attending to this combination of symbols reveals a profound teaching. To listen we must open our hearts, attending to all that we hear with compassion and a regard for the innate nobility in all beings.

The Chinese character that arose spontaneously during meditation guided me as I continued on my journey of transformation. Each week I would focus on a particular symbol of the character, integrating the image into my heart-breath meditation. I found that embracing my inner chatter with compassion during meditation allowed me to withhold my judgments and negative projections. I could observe the stories that arose from my ingrained social conditioning, refocusing my awareness on how I felt rather than what I thought. This is what Tenzin Wangyal Rinpoche meant when he wrote, "Shift your attention from the story you are telling yourself about what is happening to the inward experience." Gradually, distracting noises – my ticking bedroom clock, the barking dog next door, and my own clamoring mind – faded into the background.

Through my inner listening I began to notice another sound that lay beneath all the cacophony. This new sound was imbued with a vibration that felt comforting and calming, like the gentle hum of a loving mother. All sounds and thoughts merged, flowing through me without becoming disturbing or disruptive. My physical body and my cognitive awareness became separate from my conditioned identity. I felt one with my authentic self, a deep and essential aspect of my being, a direct antenna to the vibrations and energy flowing through the universe.

After attuning to the sounds within, I then focused my attention on how I perceived the world. With eyes open, I experimented with different gazes, playing with my new ability to observe images without grasping. I noticed that as my gaze softened and relaxed, my field of perception expanded in width, depth and clarity. Closing my eyes, I practiced my inner gaze. I began to see flickering lights and images of my organs, vessels and bones. Light cascaded down by body, extending outward into a matrix that joined with the physical environment. Years later, I recalled this experience when I encountered the intricate paintings of human energy fields by the artist Alex Gray.[44]

As my meditation practice deepened, solid boundaries that outlined the physical world began to dissolve. Entering the invisible realm of energy waves, I moved beyond my conditioned identity, reveling in the recognition of my authentic self, which was composed of pure energy and light. This experience recalled Jack Kornfield's statement, "When we shift attention from experience to the space consciousness that knows, wisdom arises."[45] In the sacred space is a radiant presence embedded with the wise information of our true nature.

One afternoon, while walking near my home in the San Gabriel Mountains, my meditative consciousness emerged spontaneously with my surroundings. Various sounds enveloped me, forming a unified vibrational energy. My vision altered as the leaves on the trees came alive and danced in the breeze. The flowers smiled and the shrubs emitted a soft glow. Gazing upward I beheld filaments of light forming strange and peculiar shapes that dissolved into the sunlight. I soon learned that I was observing energy fields, what Tibetan monks call *tigles*, or spheres of light.

This marvelous experience awakened memories from my childhood when I observed similar phenomenon gazing into the sky on my rooftop in Hong Kong. Back then my visions evoked fear and distrust. But during my walk near my home, I wept tears of joy and gratitude, for I could now exuberantly participate in the interconnectedness of all creation.

Despite my initial excitement, the frightened girl on the rooftop re-emerged, instilling an apprehension to disclose these strange experiences to others. Fortunately, the wisest and strongest part of me knew I must inform

---

44 www.alexgrey.com
45 Kornfield, J. *Meditation for Beginners*, 2008, p. 37.

Terumichi and Linda of my fantastical visions. My intuition was rewarded when my dear friends declared my capacity to experience vibrational energy and light as a *siddhi*, a gift or ability that could arise during deep meditation (see Chapter 8). They cautioned me, however, not to grasp or attach to such experiences, but to merely acknowledge and rejoice in them as they arose.

Terumichi commented, "Maybe it is time you begin formal meditation training so you can stabilize your experiences." Sensing my hesitation he added, "Buddhist teachings are a wonderful system for understanding the human condition, especially suffering. In fact, the Dalai Lama has often stated that Buddhism is a science of mind, not a religion."

THE ESSENCE OF BUDDHIST PSYCHOLOGY

My studies began with an introduction to the Four Noble Truths, the heart of the Buddha's teachings. In chapter one, we followed Prince Siddhartha on his journey of awakening. The Four Noble Truths were Siddhartha's first teaching as the Buddha (see Chapter 1).

FIRST TRUTH: Suffering exists. All humans, inevitably and without exception, will suffer.

SECOND TRUTH: The cause of suffering is our ignorance of our true nature as complete and whole. This gives rise to anger and attachment.

THIRD TRUTH: A solution exists to the problem of suffering.

FOURTH TRUTH: The path to end suffering is attained through meditation.

The First Truth is simple and straightforward. Suffering exists. Human existence will inevitably bring challenges, disappointments, physical deterioration and loss. We will fall ill, age, and die. Tragedies will occur. We will experience loss. The Second Noble Truth illuminates the cause of our suffering. Humans possess an insatiable attachment to comfort and security. This causes us to grasp for or cling to what most readily feels safe and familiar, while rejecting what is disruptive or painful. The source of our grasping and attachment is *ignorance* of our true nature, the authentic, unchanging self that exists beyond fear and our social conditioning.

This ignorance informs our reactions to challenging experiences. When we encounter hardship, rather than turn inward to search for meaning and hidden sources of strength and resolve – the wisdom and tenacity of our true nature – we often look outside of ourselves, pursuing what is safe, known and expected. This throws us into an endless cycle of suffering known as samsara. Simply stated, samsara is an existence built on the deluded view that material wealth, social status and attainment of the elusive "if only" will bring us the peace and contentment we so desperately seek.

The Third Noble Truth states that we can end our suffering. To accomplish this we must first accept that life is *impermanent*, and the only permanence is our unchanging essence. When we understand that in our human condition, change is constant and certainty does not exist, we learn to abandon our abiding fear of loss, unexpected setbacks, physical deterioration, even death. The next step requires us to acknowledge that life is *precious*, that we must be present and awake in every moment, and connect to our true nature.

The Fourth Noble Truth teaches that the path to end suffering is gained through meditation. Buddhist meditation practices serve to loosen the grip of our deluded beliefs, what the Dalai Lama calls "a fundamental misapprehension of the nature of reality,"[46] so we can hear the call of our own inner wisdom and awaken to our true nature. Meditation provides us with the means to move beyond our fundamental misapprehensions to uncover our most authentic self.

---
46 Dalai Lama. *My Life In Forbidden Lhasa*, 1955.

However, we are not all ready to accept the reality of suffering and its potential for providing wisdom and transformation.

***

Both Western and Buddhist psychology recognize the importance of developing a healthy sense of self. Both recognize how we seek to avoid pain and maximize comfort. These two theoretical approaches differ, however, in their explanations about what causes suffering and restores emotional balance. Western psychology proposes that human suffering is rooted in our inability to feel adequate or worthy. Buddhist psychology views suffering as a separation from our true nature, leaving us adrift and primed to cling to our conditioned identities and material comforts. These differing perspectives, then, support different responses to suffering.

Western psychology does little to define mental health.[47] Its theories focus on describing and categorizing mental pathology, its interventions on curing and fixing. The western model attempts to correct or manage suffering using strategies designed to change negative thoughts and behaviors promote self-esteem and personal empowerment, and improve how we manage our day to day functioning. Buddhist psychology, however, teaches us to allow, accept suffering and to experience pain. The Buddhist framework asserts that suffering arises not from the occurrence of life's inevitable challenges, but from our reactions to those challenges. When we respond to difficulty through our conditioned identity we believe the misapprehension that we are inadequate and separate from our true nature. Buddhism provides an alternative perspective, a view that invites us to look inward, to directly experience our pain through the eyes of our compassionate witness, who, even in our darkest hour, shines a light on our divine perfection.

***

---

47 Siegel, D. *The Developing Mind*, 1999.

As I contemplated the Four Noble Truths, I came to understand how my own deep pain after Gary's suicide opened my heart to compassion and cosmic consciousness. I realized that my distorted beliefs about being perfect and denying my own needs created a false self. Although asserting my personal power seemed to ignite a chain of tragic reactions, it also awakened me to my true nature.

Immediately following Gary's death, I became engulfed in my own shame and guilt. To avoid being consumed by my devastating emotions I clung to old patterns of coping. Yet, how could I rely on my conditioned beliefs when they no longer proved true? How could someone perfect, good and kind cause her own husband's suicide? Emotionally depleted, I collapsed into a cycle of panic and insomnia, further eroding my capacity to function. Overcome by the frenzied energy of Samsara, I surrendered, reaching out to Terumichi who joined me in attending the meditation gathering that would forever change my life.

Although I continued to succumb to guilt and despair at times, through meditation I could recognize these emotions as separate from my authentic self. After experiencing cosmic consciousness, I could view the experiences of my life from a place of peace and calm. Meditation and mindful listening rerouted my ingrained, conditioned patterns of thinking and feeling, prodding me ever closer towards integration and wholeness.

The precious reality of the Four Noble Truths crystalized one afternoon while viewing a broadcast about a Tibetan Buddhist nun who had been imprisoned and raped by soldiers. Although she suffered unimaginable cruelty, the nun responded with an open heart, expressing compassion and forgiveness toward her captors. Her eyes reflected a radiance and inner calm undisturbed by her incomprehensible trauma. The nun did not deny her suffering, which she spoke of through tears. But beneath her sadness there existed a sense of serenity and stillness. Rather than identify with the horror of her experience, the nun chose to view her tragedy through her inner light of compassion.

Suffering exists. Atrocities and senseless tragedies do occur. *However, our reactions to our pain can either evolve from our conditioned identities, the part of us that seeks only comfort and control, or we can respond from our radiant and compassionate heart, opening us to our truest and most authentic selves.*

TAMING THE CHAOTIC MIND

Like many beginners to meditation, I believed that I would learn to empty my mind of all thoughts and distractions. In fact, just the opposite proved true. During my initial sessions, I felt bombarded by thoughts filled with useless information. However, the more I practiced, the more easily I could allow my thoughts to drift into my awareness without judgment and without focusing on or pushing away their content. I felt as though I could place my thoughts on a lotus petal, and then, returning to my breath, watch as they floated away on a gentle, steady stream. In our day-to-day life we are often barraged with information, most of which we ignore. This onslaught of chaotic stimuli, however, causes our mind to flit about, from one thought to another, like a monkey swinging through the trees. To tame our flitting *monkey mind* we must first learn to be mindful, to be present in each moment, without clinging to or pushing away the thoughts that come and go.

Mindfulness meditation teaches us to focus on the present moment – the here and now – so we may witness our experience unfold like a story. As we observe our inner story, we suspend all judgment, no clinging to the aspects that we like and desire, nor rejecting what scares or disturbs us. Suspending our judgment, however, can prove very challenging. Since birth we are conditioned to view our experiences in a particular way that is both powerful and often unconscious. Jon Kabat-Zinn states that mindfulness "includes an affectionate, compassionate quality within the attending, a sense of openhearted, friendly presence and interest."[48] This openhearted friendliness allows us to witness our thoughts and emotions without reaction or emotional identification. We can disengage from the habitual reactions that reinforce our deluded beliefs.

---

48 *Calming Your Anxious Mind*, 2003, p.145-146.

This ability to observe without judgment helps us to cultivate the objectivity and clarity vital to emotional healing and personal growth.

Neuroscience has affirmed the role of meditation as a pathway through suffering. The discoveries of *neural plasticity* and *neurogenesis*[49] have revealed how meditation can alter the anatomical structures and biological functions of our brain. Neural plasticity is the brain's ability to alter physically in response to an experience. Neurogenesis refers to the brain's ability to manufacture new neurons and new neuronal connections in response to outside stimuli. Davidson, a pioneer in the study of mindfulness meditation, determined that Buddhist monks possess a greater activation of high-frequency gamma waves during deep meditation.[50] Gamma waves are associated with neural connections that advance our ability to integrate information and to achieve a heightened sense of awareness. In short, gamma waves promote cognitive clarity and an expanded perception of reality.

Yet, the most remarkable feature of gamma waves is their effect on our left prefrontal cortex, the section of our brain responsible for positive thoughts and emotions. Davidson found that in deep states of meditation, the left prefrontal cortex displays a high level of electrical stimulation, creating experiences of joy and contentment. Fortunately, we do not need to join a Buddhist monastery to enjoy the benefits of gamma waves. Sara Lazar[51] determined that as few as thirty minutes a day of mindfulness meditation resulted in significant increases in the cortical thickness of the brain associated with attention, sensory processing, body regulation, emotional balance, communication, awareness, intuition, and empathy, all functions and attributes necessary for contentment and well-being.

Mindfulness meditation, then, integrates neural activity and promotes a coherent state of mind. When our brain functions with integration and coherence we experience calm and contentment. We can observe our varied thoughts

---

49 Begley, S. Ibid. 2007, p.52.
50 Davidson, R. *The Emotional Life of your Brain*, 2005.
51 Lazar, S. 2005. www.nmr.mgh.harvard.edu.

and emotions without overreacting or flipping our lids. We can respond to crises and challenges with greater equanimity and an expanded perspective.[52]

***

My easy familiarity with Buddhism seemed somehow innate, as though my genetic code was uniquely suited to integrate its wisdom and practices. My intuition proved accurate; for my mother, who initially regarded my interest in meditation as alarming, disclosed that my paternal grandmother had been a devout Buddhist with a dedicated meditation practice. My mother's revelation deepened my connection to my emerging spirituality. As if guided by my grandmother's devotion, I suddenly felt called to attend a Buddhist psychology seminar at Esalen in Big Sur. Reserving my space marked the completion of a decade long yearning to study at this mecca of the human potential movement. Ten years prior, fear of losing my rational self thwarted any inclination to visit Esalen, the mecca of the human potential movement. Now, however, the opportunity to fulfill this long awaited adventure filled me with joyful anticipation.

When the day to leave finally arrived, I patiently slogged through Friday afternoon traffic. Once out of Los Angeles, the drive up the California coastline felt sublime and restorative. I checked in and took a long walk along the water, mesmerized by the dance of orange, gold and purple on the horizon. Despite the magical setting, or maybe because of it, I was at once beset by a profound sadness. Caught in an avalanche of regrets and 'what-ifs,' I succumbed to a dormant grief for the young woman whose life had been ruled by others' needs and expectations.

Rather than spiral into a vortex of black emotions, I engaged in what I had so diligently practiced during meditation. Neither grasping nor rejecting my thoughts and emotions, I observed my pain with loving awareness, noting the intensity of my sadness and regret. I witnessed the tide of my emotions subsiding

---

52 Siegel, D. 2005. See Appendix II for detailed description of mindfulness meditation and changes in the brain.

then dissolving into the boundless sky. As my breath synchronized with the gently crashing waves on the shore, I became conscious of the uncertainty and guilt I had been carrying about attending the seminar, sentiments echoed by my mother, who had questioned my choice to leave the children when I left them in her care just hours before.

Unaccustomed to spending time alone, I wondered what other demons would surface during the weekend. For the first time since my awakening, I felt uncertain about being present with my pain, and my chattering mind yearned for the bliss of ignorance. I mustered my courage, allowing the uncertainty to flow into my awareness. I took a deep breath, labeled my emotion as 'fear,' and settled into my heart-breath meditation. Realizing the true gift of turning inward, I felt my body relax and my mind grow clam.

Esalen's evening program began with a relaxation meditation. I felt acutely conscious of the tightness in my shoulders and the knot in my stomach. I followed the gentle voice of the instructor, becoming aware of the tension I held throughout my body. I connected to my breath, focusing on that part of me that carried my need to be responsible and my fear of failure. My tension began to dissolve as I surrendered to a sensation of weightlessness, as if floating on the ocean floor.

Vibrational energy enveloped me, descending through my crown and flowing throughout my body. What physical tension remained had evaporated. My rapidly beating heart settled into a gentle rhythm. All at once, I became one with a love that was as immense as it was unfathomable. In an instant, I became the poetry of William Blake. I was the "World in a Grain of Sand, and Heaven in a wild flower."

I remained in this blissful state until faint noises returned me to the room. I sat motionless in my chair, unable to move or speak. The group was engrossed in discussion that prompted one man to become irate, triggering another person's agitation at the disrupted peace. Within seconds, the room filled with tension. Suddenly, a woman's calm voice spoke to the irate man, assuring him that she understood his struggles and knew that his apparent hostility was in truth, deep anguish. The man's face softened and the room became still again. I realized that the man was, in fact, looking at me. "Thank you for listening," he said. In utter astonishment I realized that the calming feminine voice had come from me! The woman sitting next to me leaned in and whispered, "You sounded like Kuan Yin."

As a child, I had learned of Kuan Yin from our servants, who prayed to her for health and fortune. I had dismissed this goddess, whose name meant 'Observing Sound,' as Chinese superstition. Yet, somehow, my deepening connection to cosmic consciousness unlocked a portal to this loving deity whose compassion had so quickly restored calm to the room. Later I would learn that my Buddhist grandmother had consecrated a shrine to Kuan Yin in her home.

From that moment at Esalen I embraced Kuan Yin as my spiritual mother. This profoundly personal relationship with a divine mother began to transform my relationship with my human mother. I noted the shift one evening while out to dinner. As usual, before we opened our menus, my mother began her litany of complaints. Rather than reacting to her negativity and pessimism, however, I listened to my mother's words with compassion. Quite uncharacteristically, she ceased her complaining and asked me about my weekend plans.

"I'm taking a few days off from work to go to the beach by myself," I replied.

"What? You're leaving the children alone again? If it is work and training, that is okay, but you cannot take time just for fun. They need you."

Her remarks rekindled the guilt I had felt going to Esalen. As I listened to my mother's words and my own emotional reaction, I felt compassion for both my mother and myself. I observed my own annoyance, calming myself by initiating my heart-breath and refocusing my awareness. My reply emerged organically. "Mom, I love you very much, and I enjoy taking you out to dinner. But when you ask me about my plans and then criticize my decisions, I feel hurt and angry."

I spoke with the same voice from Esalen, embodying a presence that understood suffering and responded with kindness and loving wisdom. My mother stopped eating and stared at the wall. I waited for her customary avalanche of defensiveness and hurt. "I was just trying to help. I don't mean to criticize," she said haltingly, her eyes avoiding mine. "I'm glad you told me."

Stunned by my mother's response, all that I could say was, "Thanks, Mom."

An awkward silence hung between us as I wondered what would happen next. With an open heart, I took a deep breath and reached for my mother's hand. "I don't tell you enough how much I love you," I said. "And I appreciate all you have done."

"You're going to make me cry," she replied, waving her hand as if to signal the end of the conversation. She switched topics, one of her many tales of the week. I saw her lips move, but I could not hear her words. For the first time I saw my mother as an ordinary woman, filled with struggles, dreams, and disappointments. When I was young, my mother never scooped me up into her arms. We never cuddled or sang lullabies together. But, at that moment, what never happened didn't matter.

I gazed at the sixty-seven-year-old woman before me, her brown hair graying, her skin still luminous and smooth. For so much of my life, I ached for my mother's approval and understanding. Yet I had never acknowledged her pain, nor understood all that she had sacrificed. By opening to compassion and listening with my heart, I transformed many years of hurt and disappointment into unconditional love.

PART TWO THE PATH

REFLECTION

To venture within, love must be awakened.
Do you practice self-compassion?
Do you connect to a loving presence?
Take a few minutes each day to sit and listen with your heart.
Reflect on the Chinese symbol for "listen."
Allow whatever arises. Breathe.
Take time to ask yourself, "Am I listening with an open heart?
Is my breath filled with compassionate awareness?"
When judgments or distorted thoughts arise, note them and
allow them to dissolve back into the space beyond your awareness.
If distorted thoughts do not dissolve, try to listen to their messages.
Always return to the warm breath of compassion.
Keep a journal of your experiences.

CHAPTER SIX
Riding the Waves of Emotion: Integration towards Wholeness

A whole person is one who has both walked with God and wrestled with the devil.
C. G. Jung

Do you have the patience to wait till your mud settles and the water is clear? Can you remain unmoving until the right action arises by itself?
Lao-Tsu

When asked what inspired her to devote her life to God, Mother Teresa replied that it was the moment that she realized she had a 'Hitler' in her heart. After realizing the enormous human capacity for cruelty, she turned her attention toward cultivating loving compassion for the poor and destitute. She recognized that the demon inside her coexisted with the divine. It is vital to embrace both, and choose which aspect to develop. For Jung, a whole person is one who is connected to the spiritual essence, and brings awareness to the darkness, which he named *the shadow* aspect – our thoughts, feelings and experiences that we deemed as negative – in order to heal our wounds.

These disowned, powerful aspects, which reside deep within our unconscious minds, when denied or rejected, can drive us toward instinctual, habitual behaviors. For an aggressive, angry person, vulnerability or love can be dangerous, therefore, repressed into the shadow. The accepted behaviors would be those arising from aggression. For someone like me, who identified myself as a kind person, residing in my shadow was a cauldron of seething anger and other emotions, which in the West, can fall under the seven deadly sins: *lust, greed, gluttony, sloth, wrath, envy,* and *pride,* which as a child I had tried to repudiate and avoid. The origin of the word *sin* is *'missing the mark of our true essence,'* which is similar to Buddhism's *ignorance,* one of the three poisons described in the previous chapter. When we are ignorant of and disconnected from our original wholeness and essential self, we perceive and act from our fears and inadequacies, thus avoiding what is dangerous and grasping what is safe and comforting.

Crisis shatters our perceived reality and challenges us to expand our worldview to understand and transform our suffering. When we neither push away nor identify with a reaction, we can enter into a mindful state that is calm and wiser than our reactive mind. In the stillness of the moment, we can nourish the seed of spacious awareness, which is the source of wisdom, and transcend our primal, instinctual nature. *Both are hardwired into our human existence.* To promote healing, which is a sense of wholeness, we must connect with both, and allow our *shadow* and reactive aspects to have a place in our consciousness, as if they are being invited to participate in a sacred feast. By being held in this compassionate space, our instinctual selves can be accepted and honored as part of our humanness. This is what Lao-Tzu means when he asks whether we *have the patience to wait until [the] mud settles and the water is clear.* If we are still and non-reactive, *the right action [will arise] by itself* from the wisdom space.

According to Jung, the way into the unconscious "begins where emotions are generated."[53] Human emotions are instinctive, involuntary reactions that possess a powerful, elemental force that can take over the rational aspect of our consciousness – metaphorically flipping our lids, as you learned in Chapter Two. The word 'emotion' is derived from the Latin verb *motere,* which means 'to move.' Therefore, *emotions* connote movement and energy. Jung posited that

---

53 Jung, C.G. *Analytical Psychology: Its Theory and Practice,* 1968, p.487.

human emotion is a form of energy, which, with sufficient force, can disrupt the stasis or stability of our egoic self. However, emotions can *also* open a door to explore the hidden messages imbedded in the unconscious, which can greatly aid us in feeling whole. As you learned in Chapter Two, mind is intricately related to patterns of *energy* and *information* flow. *Thus, becoming aware of, and being with our emotions can affect the states of our mind, and our well being.*

Buddhism uses the metaphor of the rider and the horse in order to help us understand how the force of emotions moves us in one direction or another. The human rider represents our consciousness and the horse symbolizes our instinctual energy, or what Buddhists call *prana,* or *lung.* Typically, we become the wild horse of our emotions, which takes us wherever it wants to go. According to the teachings, in order to stay on the path of awareness, we need to tame the wild horse (the instinctual energy) of our psyche, and learn to guide it where *we* want it to go through cultivating the rider consciousness. If the rider is not aware of the energy of the horse, then he or she will not be able to steer it in a positive direction. The result is a 'runaway horse' that gallops wildly about, without seeing where it's going, crashing into trees, stepping into holes, or running around in circles, getting nowhere.

If we allow ourselves to become enslaved by the wild horse of our emotions we are likely to become reactive and flip our lids, resulting in chaos. An experienced equestrian, like my daughter Jennifer, knows that she cannot force the horse into submission, but with patient attention to the needs of the horse, she can eventually calm it down and teach it to move along the peaceful path in nature. In time, like a horse whisperer, the rider melds with the horse and they flow together, with the horse responding to the gentle commands of the rider, without prodding.[54]

It took a long time, but eventually I learned to tame the initial wild horse of shock, shame and guilt that erupted from the crisis. Through meditation, my nervousness and anxiety were transformed into an inner feeling of peace and

---

[54] For an example of this, see the excellent documentary, *Buck,* the subject of Robert Redford's film, *The Horse Whisperer.*

calm. However, the insight I gained through meditation gave me a naïve sense of confidence that I had become an expert rider of my emotions, and convinced me that I would now be free of negative thoughts and instinctual, knee-jerk reactions. In my innocence, I thought this beginner's meditation would bring me transcendence and liberate me forever from my suffering. Beginners to meditation often fall into this trap of what the noted Tibetan Buddhist teacher, Chögyam Trungpa, calls the 'pitfall of spiritual materialism.'

This pitfall is the expectation of immediately finding a higher, transcendent self that is devoid of any negative traits. But as Trungpa would say, enlightenment does not come that easily. According to him, in order to take the first step to spiritual development, "we must surrender our hopes and expectations, as well as our fears, and march directly into our disappointment."[55] We cannot bypass our human pain by becoming 'spiritual.' In fact, when we awaken and become more spacious and aware, the hidden, repressed files of our human story can now come to the surface to be healed. Without fully understanding this wisdom, I had naïvely used my spiritual practice to fortify my ego identity in an attempt to 'bypass' the negative traits I wanted to disown. Paradoxically, it was through the experience of finding love that I encountered my inner Hitler, which shook me to my core and made me realize that I was far from taming the wild horse of my emotions.

***

As my meditation practice gave me a feeling of stability and joy, I began to open to a world beyond being a single mother and widow. Despite my trepidation, I agreed to a blind date, arranged by a good friend. To my surprise, Paul was a wonderful, attentive man, who made me laugh. For the first time, I felt appreciated, nurtured, and immensely happy. Most important, I felt *safe* with him. After a few months of dating, I introduced Paul to my children, who adored him. He played with them, cooked for us, and brought laughter to a

---

55 Trungpa, C. *Spiritual Materialism*, 1986, p.108.

home that had been severely shaken by painful memories. Filled with hope, I thought this was a chance to find happiness and security, an opportunity to begin anew.

The security of love allowed my shadow to come to the surface, and a minor misunderstanding between Paul and me escalated into an argument. A surge of anger and jealousy erupted within me. Suddenly, as if under a spell, I unleashed a torrent of hateful words at Paul, who I thought had disappointed and therefore betrayed me. The enormous force of my rage surprised and frightened me. In that moment, I realized that I had a huge reservoir of anger hidden within me. I was unnerved by my reaction, and was thrown into a state of panic. The emotional avalanche of this argument forced me to face my rage, and try to understand its source.

This ferocious rage also called into question my perceived identity as a kind and loving person. My Catholic upbringing reinforced the sensitive being in me, who was acutely aware of others' suffering. On weekends and summers, I volunteered at health clinics for the poor, which were located in the small islands near Hong Kong. As I cleansed and bandaged their wounds, I felt a tremendous sense of love pouring from my heart. I saw this work as a reflection of my faith, and I considered my service and self-sacrifice as an important part of my core identity. Having felt the terror of my father's rage, I strongly identified with these suffering victims, and naïvely believed that I should never hurt others through anger.

As a result, I learned to suppress my anger and other *sins*, and always defer to authority figures in order to avoid confrontation. I saw myself as a caretaker and repressed any personal feelings of disappointment or injustice, pushing them into the shadow of my unconscious. With my crisis initiation, many of my illusions and psychological defenses that had served me in the past began to crumble into dust. Although mystical experiences through meditation had dissolved my sense of guilt and deep depression, I was unaware of the rage that boiled inside me. Feeling safe and loved, this repressed wrathful aspect about injustice and betrayal finally erupted.

PART TWO THE PATH

The rage that I experienced in my relationship with Paul was part of what Jung calls an *emotional complex*. The 'complex' of human emotions is built up over a lifetime, beginning with birth or even earlier. Developmental psychologists recognize that, by the end of the first year, a child has formed an adaptive perspective, which is shaped by its personal experiences that are filtered through the child's unique temperament. The early phase of the child's development is particularly important, because trauma and other experiences of extreme suffering are capable of causing damage to one's sense of self. The result of these injuries is what Jung calls *complexes*, which are emotionally charged groups of ideas or images. According to Jung, these complexes, like files in the computer, collect energy from trauma and perceived injuries, which reinforces our habitual, instinctual negative reactions. When activated and opened, these complex files of our stories unleash their viral energy and override the commands of other 'files.' These complex files heavily influence what we deem as unacceptable, and whatever we reject gets pushed into our shadow. Without awareness, we are in danger of becoming possessed by our complexes and enslaved by our emotions. In other words, we let the wild horse take us where it wants to go.

In order to ride the waves of our emotions and tame the wild horse of our psyches, we must first bring awareness to the proceedings. In the light of this awareness we are able to observe these inner thoughts and feelings and allow them to gradually *discharge* their powerful energy. The process of connecting to the light of awareness involves two vital steps. The first step is to *recognize* our shadows as they arise, and bring awareness to the contents of our complexes. The second step is to coordinate and integrate – make whole – the fragmented, chaotic darkness of these shadows. By being in stillness, we can compassionately observe our negative thoughts and feelings, and allow them to release their tremendous amount of energy, which, if given enough time, will *eventually* dissipate, leaving us calm and collected. However, in order to *contain* this raw, instinctual energy, one must first learn to create a strong and viable vessel.

A STRONG CONTAINER

Meditation alone could not dissolve the force of my rage, which took over and unleashed angry accusations at Paul. Although he was incredibly patient and understanding of my outbursts, I felt totally out of control. I knew I needed additional support, which I found through my initial interest in Jung's teachings when I was in graduate school. At that time I was unable to comprehend his concepts, so I set aside his writings and returned to my conventional studies. After my initiation through crisis, I rekindled my connection with Jung, who was referenced in one of my Buddhist books. When my rage erupted as a result of an argument with Paul, I had been reading Jung's autobiography, *Memories, Dreams, and Reflection*. His writings helped me understand this explosive emotion, place it in context, and regard it as an opportunity to gain a glimpse into a powerful complex.

A dream helped me decide my next step. In the dream I was climbing a steep mountain and could see a plateau not far ahead where I could rest. Exhausted and unable to pull myself up, I was beginning to panic when someone grabbed my outstretched hand. When I looked up, I saw it was Jung. Through the dream, my subconscious was telling me that Jung's ideas would help me face my demons and alleviate my suffering. I decided to enter Jungian analysis, and went to an analyst that an acquaintance recommended. Conveniently, Ann lived close-by, a twenty-minute walk from my house.

At our first meeting, Ann, a kind, compassionate, silver-grey haired woman greeted me at the door to her office with a gentle smile. After polite introductions, she asked me to 'share something about myself.' I wasn't sure where to begin, but feeling safe, I soon found myself opening my heart to this complete stranger about the horror of Gary's psychotic breakdown and suicide. I described to her my spiritual awakening and explained how my feelings of jealousy and anger had surfaced. Proudly and confidently, I announced to Ann, "I am here to work hard, and uncover *all* of my shadows, so I will not be rageful anymore."

I was more than a bit chagrined when she informed me that the shadows of our psyches could never be *fully* revealed or known. With these words, I felt my innards twist and my composure began to crumble. I had naïvely thought I was going to confront my rage, release its negative energy, and in a very short time, feel completely whole again. Now, Ann was telling me that I could never uncover all aspects of my shadows, so where did that leave me? As I sat with her, I began to feel an overwhelming sense of anxiety, as if she could see right through me, to my needy, damaged self, who forgot her radiant essence. Doubts crept in, and I began to wonder if I could actually heal this underlying anxiety, which I realized was a profound sense of shame.

Alice Miller, a child psychoanalyst, describes the phenomenon of *forbidden suffering,* when children are not permitted by parents or society to express their pain at being wounded.[56] She believes that the trauma itself will cause injury, but what is more devastating to the child is the confusion and despair over the inability to give expression to the suffering and receive the reassurance and soothing that he or she needs. If the suffering is forbidden, the underlying emotional turmoil will then be repressed until it erupts in some negative form later in life. These early insidious traumas can result in an indescribable dread that one will be annihilated, which Heinz Kohut called *disintegration anxiety.*[57] In my desperation to heal this wounded aspect, the one whose pain had been suppressed for so many years, I had forgotten the teachings of the Second Noble Truth. I lost my connection to the light and identified with the shame of being angry. I became attached to the notion of healing through disowning and rejecting my pain. For the first time since my awakening, I felt challenged to dive deeper into my interior world. But first, I had to reconnect with my compassionate witness and the wisdom of realizing my reactions were not my true nature.

Despite my fears and doubts, I returned weekly to explore my unconscious realm with Ann. I became painfully aware of an overwhelming dread

---

56 Miller, A. *Forbidden Suffering,* 1983.
57 Kohut, H. *The Analysis of the Self,* 1971.

at speaking ill of my parents and a sense that I was complaining about minor problems. Under Ann's guidance, I learned to hold space for my anxious, shameful aspects, and utilize active imagination, a Jungian method, as a way to bring consciousness to the raw energy that was consuming me. Similar to Buddhist practices, Jung believed that one has to approach the unconscious and its shadow from a place of non-judgment with openness to discover and explore its contents. From this place of compassion, I was able to objectively observe the tension I held in my body and my mind.

Intuitively, I knew that I needed to focus my active imagination on my *body*, by identifying where I was holding the tension. I immediately noticed a tight, gnawing sensation in my stomach and chest. Initially, this feeling was overwhelming, and I wanted to push it away in order to escape. Instead, I asked the anxious energy in my stomach to express itself as a color or symbol. To my surprise, the frenzied sensation turned into a black, swirling vortex. As I continued to breathe calmly, observing this vortex, its vibrations began slowly to subside. The swirling energy morphed into that of a young girl, who huddled in the corner of the room, trembling from the fear of being seen. I was amazed to encounter this terrified part of myself, and gently began to talk to her. With patience, I was able to communicate with this little frightened girl, and calm her down.

These experiences were like threads that I took each week to Ann, and together we wove a tapestry of my wholeness. Her calmness and compassion were essential to my capacity to keep diving into the depths and shed the amour that protected my vulnerable self. It took many weeks to become comfortable and familiar with the images and sensations that were arising from my unconscious. Each week, I became increasingly aware of the scared little girl within me, and her pattern of frenzied energy. I noticed how when I could hold space for her to *be*, and embrace her with unconditional love and compassion, the frenetic energy gradually dissipate. The compassionate witness became a powerful container that stabilized the buzzing, free-floating anxiety of this little frightened girl, whose suffering had been forbidden until now. The ability to witness and ride the waves of anxiety cleared the dense energy, and expanded my perspective to see the whole story. It was as if I had become an audience member, watching a play unfold, seeing how the protagonist would extricate herself from this tragedy. This ability to witness and contain was the same experience I felt when I cradled my daughter, who erupted into a state of anxiety during an innocent game of marbles (see Chapter 4).

With time, I learned to hold what Jung called 'the tension of opposites.' This means learning to contain one's conflicting sensations by creating an open space, which neither pushes away the fear, anger, or confusion, nor succumbs to it. By allowing the forbidden suffering to surface, the fearful part of me began to come alive during one of my journaling processes, and I began to dialogue with her. "Why are you so anxious?" I asked. In almost a whisper, she answered, "It's because something is wrong with me. I am no good. I'm unlovable." After a pause, she added, "I don't matter. No one really wants me. So it is safer to be invisible." Immediately, I felt the contraction in my throat and stomach. Beneath the anxiety was a layer of thick shame, as if I were damaged and unworthy of love. The only safe place was to hide behind the mask of being kind and subservient. With a flash of insight, I saw this frightened child as the *matchstick girl,* the little orphan in the fairy tale who was left alone in the world, and sold matchsticks to survive. She would stare into the window of a loving family, yearning to be included, but fearful to be noticed. For the matchstick girl, it was safer to be in the familiar, freezing cold than reside in the warmth of a family, who might discover how bad she was and reject her.

By retrieving my fragmented memories of this little girl and her feelings of inadequacy and abandonment, I began to make sense of how much my needs had been denied and dismissed. I was the humble matchstick girl when my mother asked me to sacrifice my love of learning so as not to hurt my brother's feelings. However, like other children, the matchstick girl needed to be seen, loved and reassured. Calmly observing the matchstick girl, I realized this shadow aspect was carrying the gnawing pain of emptiness at having been discounted, ignored, and neglected. She was the incredible tightness in my belly, the tightness in my throat, the shortness in my breath. For the first time, I clearly witnessed my pain, and my great fear of annihilation, which I realized was not only experienced by me alone. These are universal human emotions that arise when we are disconnected from our wholeness.

By bringing awareness to this fearful, shame-filled little girl, I began to piece together my past wounded behavior, including the bulimic episodes that I had pushed aside. The seemingly crazy and shameful behavior – binging and purging in response to anxiety – now seemed understandable. Given the circumstances, I understood my reactions to the stress of feeling unsafe around Gary. As a subservient wife who had no voice in our marriage, I resorted to stuffing my pain with food and then vomiting it out as a way of expressing the horror of feeling trapped by Gary's angry outbursts. With compassionate awareness, I was able to watch not only the suffering of the little girl, but also the young woman who was so lost. As I embraced both of these aspects with love, and allowed them the space to speak their truths, the emotional minefield of my anxiety and shame began to subside. With subsequent waves of the overwhelming emotions, I was equipped with the right tools to stay connected to my awareness, and was able to guide my wild, galloping horse to a calm, safe terrain.

***

When we start on the journey to awakening, we have no idea where the journey will take us. We learn to trust the unfolding and the guide. A few months following my initial encounter with the *matchstick girl*, I was taken by surprise into the deep, dark caverns of forbidden suffering. A session with Ann began innocently about the masks we all wear to hide our shame and fears, when suddenly I heard a voice within prodding me. "It is time to tell her your secret!" Despite sitting across from the compassionate presence of Ann, I was squirming in my chair and was unable to find the right words to speak the truth. As the images of my childhood secret began to rise to the surface, I was overcome with nausea. With a sigh of surrender and relief, I heard myself utter, "When I was ten, I was sexually molested."

The power of the truth stunned both of us into silence. I could not even look at Ann, but I felt her love and I could hear her breath, which was calming. "My parents weren't home, and I had gone to bed earlier than my brother and sister. I had fallen asleep, but later was awakened by a sharp pain."

I paused, hardly able to continue. With the words sticking in my mouth, I said, "Someone was touching my body. I was petrified and did not know what to do. At that moment, I could not scream out. As I slightly opened my eyes, I recognized my attacker was my servant's 15-year-old nephew. I was confused and alarmed, but for some reason I was unable to protest and stop him from digging his fingers deep inside me. I became numb, as if I were not in my body. I felt nothing, as if I were asleep." Reacting automatically to this traumatic encounter, I had gone into a 'freeze' response, unable to move or speak.[58]

"After what seemed like an eternity, he finally left. I waited a long time before I 'thawed,' and got up from bed, gingerly, and went to the bathroom to relieve myself. Although the pain was excruciating, I remained silent, even upon seeing the blood on my underwear. Robotically, I cleaned myself up, and went back to bed. Lying in bed, a disturbing thought kept reverberating in my head. My mother had warned me several times never to let any man touch me 'down there.' But, because I had allowed this boy to fondle me, I was overwhelmed with a sense of guilt and shame. I felt as if it was *my* fault that this had happened, that somehow I was to blame, and that through some super-human effort, I should have been able to prevent it. Breathing in the guilt and shame, I fell back to oblivious sleep, telling myself it was like a dream."

What amazes me to this day was my response to this molestation. Instead of raising a ruckus, the following morning I pushed aside my fears and anxieties, and confronted my servant's nephew. Faced with the fact that he might be exposed, and that his auntie would lose her job, he began to break down in tears. He begged me not to tell his aunt or my parents. Beyond the desire to

---

58 Ogden, P. *Trauma in the Body*, 2006.

avoid the shame that would arise from speaking the truth, I was filled with an inordinate sense of compassion for him, and agreed not to tell anyone, if and only if he promised never to do anything like this again, to anybody. After he consented, I forgave him, and we agreed to keep our secret.

Until this session with Ann, I had kept this promise and never told anyone about my sexual molestation. As I recounted this story to Ann, I sighed, vividly seeing this boy's anguished face. Exhaling the tension in my body, I felt more at ease and the story continued to unfold. "Despite our agreement, I became ever vigilant around him," I said. "I was obsessed with the thought that others could see that I had been defiled. I felt like damaged goods." Fortunately, a year later he left the household. But this did not assuage my irrational, naïve fear that somehow I could become pregnant. For two years I lived with the guilt and fear, watching for any signs that my belly was growing. Years later, I was relieved when I learned the facts of reproduction during a class on sex education. I went on with my life, acting as if this abuse had not affected me.

As I relived this painful experience that had been locked away for so long in the shadow of my psyche, Ann helped me gain perspective. She pointed out that by this time in my life, I had already learned to suppress my voice. I had no idea what reserves lay within this little girl that allowed her to respond so calmly to this crisis. A year earlier, when I reacted to my father's unreasonable demands by standing up for myself, I was met with his wrath. Therefore, I was acutely attuned to avoid conflict, even if it meant suppressing my needs and desires. This insight brought clarity to the decisions I had previously made in life, including my decision to marry Gary. When I could no longer push away my needs and stood up to him, he began a rapid descent into psychosis. His suicide was the beginning of my journey to awaken my authentic self, to uncover the layers of my repressed suffering and eventually feel whole again. My old beliefs had taught me to tolerate abuse, but also to discount or deny my past trauma.

PART TWO THE PATH

FACING THE DEMON'S RAGE

After becoming aware and beginning to love and accept this wounded and frightened little matchstick girl of my past, my demonic rage emerged. Months of grieving had cleared the entangled emotions of fear and guilt, and I now sensed an explosive anger in the pit of my stomach. In a series of dreams, fleeting images of a dark figure began to appear. The figure was faceless, but I could sense its intense rage, and I woke up from these nightmares with my heart pounding. One night, the demon showed her face to me. In the dream, she was a wild-haired madwoman tied up in a straitjacket, locked in a basement, screaming, and she looked at me with fiery red eyes. As I began to journal about these dreams and dialogue with the images they contained, the imagined figure came alive on paper.

"Don't ignore me," she cried out in a thunderous voice. "I am you. I am your mother and your grandmother who gave up her education when she got married." She told me that she was very old and had been living in my psyche for generations. Having been oppressed, enslaved and forgotten, she now demanded to be set free. "No, I can't let you loose," I protested. "You are mad and will hurt me." I was surprised by my temerity in facing this madwoman, yet excited to feel the power of her rage. She responded by saying, "Trust me. You are afraid only because you don't know me." Her anger softened and her wrathful face became gentler. "Come, let me loose," she said. As I was about to set her free, I felt my stomach tighten severely. "No, I am not ready yet," I told her.

With these words, our dialogue abruptly ended. The madwoman morphed into many large venomous snakes, which tried to bite me. Instinctively I flinched. I thought about escape, but I knew I needed to contain this raw, instinctual energy. At that moment, I asked for help and instantly Kuan Yin, the Chinese goddess of love and compassion, appeared and entered me. With her wisdom eyes, I was able to gaze into the demonic eyes of this madwoman, who wanted to kill and destroy everyone who had hurt and betrayed her. I recognized her as the one who had raged at Paul for disappointing her. A powerful vibration of compassion radiated from my heart, and suddenly, my fear at this raging Medusa dissolved.

By letting go of my fear and judgment, the repressed rage that was in my shadow was now given a rightful place. I took time to *listen* to the forbidden anger of generations of women in my lineage. I heard my grandmother's anguish in having to give up the school that she founded for destitute children. I heard my mother's anger at being used and betrayed by the men in her life, particularly my father. But most significantly, I witnessed my own anger at being unprotected and abused. I was enraged that I was not allowed to speak my truth, not allowed to excel in my passion to study, yet I was to be successful and accomplished. One by one, decades of undigested, silenced anguish began to surface. At times, I felt impatient with myself, considering myself to be a victim. I learned to become aware of these reactive patterns and rode on the breath of compassion, as I continued to listen, dialogue and allow. Gradually, the tsunami rage was transformed into a powerful golden nectar of truth.

Embracing this dark anger allowed me to see that the fierce rage had been present in my marriage with Gary, but she showed up as the 'ice queen,' whose silent, cold judgment and sense of superiority formed a frozen wall around my heart. I encountered the 'killer judge,' with her sharp, critical attitude of 'whatever you do is not good enough for me.' It was painful to realize that these shadow elements resided in me, but more challenging was acknowledging that at times I was possessed by these demons in my interactions with Gary. Although I was fearful of him, there were times I had been cold and judgmental as a way to protect myself. With compassion, I forgave myself for inflicting pain on Gary, as he done to me. The healing message I received from Gary's soul when I first saw Linda became clearer. Ignorant and disconnected from my essential self, I had been living life from a *reactive, survival identity.*

The more I recognized and retrieved the fragmented parts of my psyche, the stronger and more grounded I felt. Unlike during the crisis, when I was submerged in my suffering and nearly drowned by its emotional tsunami, I was now riding the waves of my forbidden grief and rage. By radically listening and cultivating a compassionate witness for this chaotic and frozen energy, I was able to heal my childhood trauma. I felt an incredible sense of lightness, both physically and mentally, as if a heavy burden had been lifted. Finally, the frozen pain of my past was beginning to thaw. *Essential to this process was accessing an inner sanctuary, which is a nonjudgmental compassionate container to hold the imbalanced energy.*

This inner sanctuary allows healing by bringing awareness to the engulfing emotional waves of trauma. The process of creating a container is not linear, and involves being open to the unknown, embracing the past with compassion, and bringing light to the dark shadows of the psyche. Gurdjieff, the Sufi mystic, said that only through self-remembering can a person awaken from a life of 'waking sleep.' To remember our authentic selves and unbind our souls, we must recollect and integrate the disowned aspects of our pasts. The pathway into our interior world, as Jung stated, is through understanding the nature of our emotions and riding their elemental force until equilibrium is reached. By stabilizing the raw force of our instinctual emotions, we can access and harness the calm, coherent vibration of transcendent states.

THE VIBRATIONAL PATTERNS OF EMOTIONS

In her groundbreaking book, *The Molecules of Emotions,* Candace Pert provides scientific evidence for the connection between mind and body.[59] She discovered that our emotions are produced by a special class of chemicals known as neuropeptides, which bind to certain receptors in the molecules. These chemical signals carry emotional information that floods our bodies and affects the flow of energy. Similar to the domino effect, emotions of fear or joy can set off a cascade of chemical reactions that alter our brain chemistry, activate the stored memory files of our past experiences, shape our perceptions and states of mind, and powerfully influence our behavior.

---

59 Pert, C. *The Molecules of Emotions,* 1997.

In addition to these chemical signals, every emotion and thought has its own unique vibration frequency pattern. Valerie Hunt, a pioneer in the study of the human energy field, was the first to measure different vibration patterns during physical illness, interactions with others, and transcendent spiritual states.[60] The various vibrations produced by these states emit different electrical charges that affect the electromagnetic fields of our cells and their environments. Other scientific research has demonstrated that *positive emotions* produce electrical charges that emit faster and higher-frequency vibrations, which result in the body feeling *lighter* and more *spacious*. *Negative emotions*, such as anger, depression, and anxiety, produce slower and lower-frequency vibrations, and sensations of *heaviness* and *density*. Positive emotions give one the feeling of spaciousness, and our white cells are filled with more calming chemicals that produce a healthy immune system. Negative emotions are experienced as constriction and trigger stressful chemicals such as cortisol in our bodies.[61]

Our emotions and thoughts activate chemicals and vibration patterns that send signals to our brain and the rest of our body, triggering chain reactions and affecting the electromagnetic fields of our cells. These include the cells in the heart, which act as a powerful transmitter and receiver of energy communication between cells, and between the cells and the environment (see Chapter Four). *Emotions are powerful energies that organize, direct, and influence our perceptions, cognition, and behavior.* Frenzied or frozen emotions can block and distort our energy fields. In order to achieve a sense of well being and harmony, we need to shift the chaotic or rigid emotional and mental energies toward a balanced state, which is central to cultivating higher states of consciousness. Bruce Ecker's recent work on unlocking the emotional brain and promoting reconsolidation of repressed memory towards coherence is part of this integrated approach to healing.[62]

---

60 Hunt, V. Ibid.
61 McCraty, R. Heartmath, www.heartmath.org
62 Ecker, B. *Unlocking the Emotional Brain*, 2012.

PART TWO THE PATH

THE QUANTUM FIELD

To understand the energy field and its relation to the transformation of consciousness, it is helpful to have a basic knowledge of quantum physics. Classical physics built its world out of two kinds of entities, matter and fields. Einstein challenged this separation of the universe with his relativity theory. He demonstrated that light exists as a bundle of energy or a quantum, and that the higher the frequency of light, the more energy in the bundle. The energy in subatomic particles is absorbed and emitted in *quanta,* or light. These energy bundles create a stable structure that becomes matter. His famous equation, $E = mc^2$, shows that *all mass is a form of energy*, which is *not solid*, and it can be transformed into other forms of energy. Einstein demonstrated the existence of a dynamic flow and interconnectedness in the subatomic universe.

Everything in the universe is made up of an energy field. This energy field consists of two qualities: particles and waves. A quantum object as energy exists initially as waves and is not manifested in ordinary reality until it is *observed* as a particle. This is known as *'the principle of the collapse of the wave.'* The observed system requires containment in order to be defined, yet within the containment there needs to be *interaction* for observation to occur. The energy in these particles or matter appears to be affected by the size of confinement. The smaller the region of space, the faster the energy will move and vibrate. Given more space, the particles are less active and more stable. This important finding regarding *the rate of vibration and space* has a profound implication for the transformation of the state of mind.

Once two quantum particles are connected, whatever happens to one will influence the other, regardless of the distance and time separating them. This is known as the *'principle of quantum action at a distance.' The particles are connected and information seems to pass through space*. Waves only manifest as particles when observed. Therefore, it implies that there are always these 'information' waves ready to manifest in ordinary reality through observation.

Physicists Hugh Everett and Bryce DeWitt posit that once something is observed, the possibilities in the waves come into existence in parallel branches.[63] Only one aspect is observed in this 'reality,' but there are many others in different worlds. *Depending on how we observe our emotions and thoughts, there is other 'information' in the emotional and mental waves ready for us to download and shift our 'reality.'*

These waves are ever-present and connected. David Bohm theorized that the universe is an *unbroken wholeness*, which implies that mind and matter are not separate realms. He posited the existence of two forms of order, *implicate* and *explicate*.[64] At the deepest 'non-manifest' implicate order these waves of energy are enfolded into thoughts and feelings. When observed and made aware, they manifest as the explicate order. Our emotions, thoughts, and symbols carry *information*, which through awareness can be manifested, and this allows us to *choose among different responses, each with a different outcome*. As you learned from Chapter 2, states of mind emerge from a pattern of *energy* and *information* flow, so when new information arises and is observed, it can modify the energy and thus change the states of mind.

Citing the neurophysiological findings of Benjamin Libet, physicist Fred Alan Wolf postulates that the 'real' history of an electron depends on what happens at the start of the trajectory and at the end.[65] The history becomes real when it has acceptable points, thus changing the storyline of our reality and consciousness. Wolf's theory may explain why we seek to make meaning of our experiences. These experiences are energetically connected on an invisible wave level, which moves in a certain trajectory until they make sense and become whole.

These scientific findings offer insight into understanding and transforming our suffering minds. Emotions, thoughts, and the cells in the physical body comprise electromagnetic fields, which are connected to a universal energy field. Transformation of frenzied or frozen energy depends on at least *two* important aspects. First, *activating the role of the observer* changes the particles and waves of

---

63 Evrett & Dewitt, *Philosophy of Quantum Mechanics*, 1977.
64 Bohm, D. *Wholeness and the Implicate Order*, 1980.
65 Wolff, Fred. A. *Mind into Matter*, 2000.

the *observed* thoughts and emotions. Second, *creating more space* provides stability to slow down the vibration of the particles, and download other information.

Science is now providing evidence for what ancient wisdom lineages have known for thousands of years: that we are interconnected in a web of energy and our individual emotions and thoughts are influenced by this collective energetic field. These findings shed light on the energy and information flow that promote healing and transformation. Jung, who attempted to bridge science and ancient wisdom, personally experienced this field, which he called the collective unconscious.

In Jung's view, both the psychic and physical worlds dissolve into pure energy and the laws of the physical realm govern the psyche, which is an open system of energy and information. Just as observation collapses the wave, which is manifested as particles in ordinary reality, our ego-consciousness opens to the unconscious and, through observation, the information waves of the archetypes manifest as images and symbols. The energy of these symbols, which Jung considered to be *numinous* in nature (that is, having a mysterious power or filled with spirit), is of a higher frequency light than that of the complexes. Jung believed that the key to psychic transformation lies in cultivating a strong observer as a container that holds the ebb and flow of our psychic energy. The container provides the space for the 'ego' to open to the unconscious and become aware of the contents underlying the emotional charge. He believed that people's instinctual natures could be transformed to reach their highest spiritual potential. Through the process of *containment* and *awareness*, the initial force serves as a spiraling wave that allows one to access and transform the underlying and unconscious roots of the original psychic injury.

Jung theorized that psychic transformation takes place when the *dense, heavier energy of the complexes is held in the vessel of the observing ego* and witnessed by a nonjudgmental self, who remains open and attentive to whatever arises. Held in a gesture of reverence rather than rejection, the instinctual energy of our emotions and thoughts can be transformed and integrated. With this energetic shift, symbols and transcendent images emerge from the unconscious and a finer light energy can contain, penetrate, and dissolve the denser energy of these complexes. The new information can also bring a sense of completeness, so the complexes creating the story line of our reality can shift as well.

Like the changes in the electron when it finds acceptable points in its course, our perception of what we hold to be reality can also be transformed by finding *new points* that make sense to us. The numinous symbols with their new wave of information can shift the story line of the complexes by introducing healing images, insights, and positive emotions. Through active imagination and dialogue with new symbols, the suffering mind that is identified with the complexes can transform. Crisis can serve as a gift of awakening, showing us how our existing beliefs are ineffective to cope with the overwhelming situation facing us. Like the mythic hero, we are challenged to transform our perceptions and embark on a journey of discovering *new points* in our story line. Perhaps the ultimate point is the realization that our perfected whole essence, which when observed, realized and integrated, enables us to embrace our human story rather than identify with it.

In the following chapter, the three pillars of compassion, radical listening and riding the waves of emotions are brought together to formulate a model of transformation from suffering to becoming our authentic essence.

THE NECTAR OF TRANSFORMED PAIN

As I became a conscious rider of my emotions and integrated my disowned shadow, my external life began to thrive. No longer fearful or judgmental toward my father, I was able to enjoy his yearly visits. I came to accept my father for who he was, and forgave him for not being the adoring, responsible father of my archetypal story. He was still a chain-smoking, alcoholic gambler, but I was now able to contain his rage with my powerful heart warrior energy, and set clear boundaries.

I also accepted my mother's tendency to be critical and anxious. Perhaps because of my openness and acceptance, she astounded me with her willingness to grow. Since our eventful dinner when I first spoke up about her critical remarks, we became closer and talked often. I felt empowered and loving. Unlike the little girl who tried to be her confidante and caretaker, I listened and held space for her story. One afternoon during a weekend visit at my place, my mother surprised me by remarking how successful and strong I had become. "I underestimated you," she said. "You really grew from the tragedy. I was afraid you would fall apart, and I was hard on you." She looked directly at me, and told me how much our conversations had helped her. "I never felt close to my mother," she said. "I was her firstborn. I realized she sacrificed so much when she was pregnant with me. All this time, I thought she rejected me, but she was rejecting being a mother." For the first time, my mother was making meaning of her story.

This authentic connection broke down the walls between us, and suddenly I found myself telling her about my molestation. My mother looked at me with tears in her eyes and reached for my hand, an act that was unfamiliar for her. "I am so sorry," she said. By sharing my pain with her, I opened up a space where my mother could reveal her pain to me. Until now, she had kept the family secrets, and her childhood traumas to herself. "My father started molesting me when I was around eleven years old," she said. For a moment, my breath froze from the shock. Then our hearts synchronized in the ocean of compassion and an indescribable warmth emerged.

I became my mother's witness as she released decades of forbidden suffering. We sat together on the very sofa where a few years before, after Gary's suicide, my mother had silenced my tears. We now held each other, and shared tears of torment, abuse, and grief for our lost childhoods. Unlike the little girl who was my mother's confidant and took on her suffering, I had become a compassionate witness, who was able to 'listen' and ride the waves of pain. At that very moment, Jennifer, the voice of the future generation of women, came bounding up the stairs. Seeing her mother and grandmother crying and holding each other, she laughed and said, "How wonderful. This is a Kodak moment!" Her innocent and truthful remark dissolved our pain, and we all started laughing, rejoicing in the triumph of the human spirit.

REFLECTION: Riding Your Waves

*With compassion and radical listening, you now can ride
the waves of your emotions.*

Continue bringing awareness when you are triggered. This creates Space.

*With Space, there is movement of the breath into your heart.
Witness and allow the energy to shift.
Know that as the frozen, or frenzied energy subsides,
your suffering state of mind can become calmer.*

If the waves become calm, then continue resting in your breath.

*Listen and allow information to arise.
Remember your innate wholeness.
Our wounds need the soothing light to enter.*

CHAPTER SEVEN

The Heart-Mind Transformation Process: An Integrated Approach

We are shaped by our thoughts; we become what we think.
When the mind is pure, joy follows like a shadow that never leaves.
Buddha

Grief can be the garden of compassion. If you keep your heart open through everything,
your pain can become your greatest ally in your life's search for love and wisdom.
Rumi

My journey of awakening following Gary's suicide returned me to the realm of cosmic consciousness and taught me how compassionate awareness could dissolve my darkness and despair. Holding fast to these gifts, I learned to recognize my habitual, conditioned patterns and ride the waves of my reactive emotions, leading me to a profound inner transformation. Bringing awareness and breath to my open heart allowed the dense energy of my suffering to soften into the luminous and spacious energy of love. As the Buddha declared, when we transform our suffering mind, we can open ourselves to the source of infinite love and awaken to our true nature.

By integrating the wisdom paths that guided me through my suffering – Jungian psychology, neuroscience, quantum physics, and Buddhism – I developed a model to help recognize our habitual reactions, bring compassion to our reactivity, and transform unclaimed aspects of ourselves so we may move towards integration and healing. The model, which I termed the Heart-Mind Transformation Process, has five steps that move from A through E in a simple mnemonic code. While each step is distinct, together they create a structure that is open and fluid rather than stepwise and linear. Applying the model promotes Siegel's description of a healthy, integrated state of mind, which is flexible, adaptive, coherent, energized, and stable (FACES).[66]

THE HEART-MIND TRANSFORMATION PROCESS

> A = Awareness
> B = Breath
> C = Compassionate Witness
> D = Describe and Dialogue to Dis-identify and Dissolve
> E = Effective and Empathic Responses

STEP 1: A = AWARENESS

The first step towards healing is *Awareness*. We cannot heal and transform what we cannot recognize, name, and acknowledge. Self-acceptance and patience are vital to cultivating awareness. The distressing thoughts, emotions and sensations of our habitual reactions cannot emerge when thwarted by our own judgment and fear. Heart-Mind awareness includes:

- recognizing our habitual reactions,
- naming the thoughts and emotions underlying our reactivity,

---

[66] Siegel, D. 2007, p.319. Nine domains: consciousness, vertical, bi-lateral, memory, narrative, state, interpersonal, temporal, and transpirational. For more details, see appendix II.

- acknowledging that our thoughts and emotions are not our true identity,
- sensing how and where our reactivity manifests in our bodies, and
- identifying who or what triggers our reactions

When we react with a negative conditioned response, we need to identify how the reactivity manifests. Do we feel a particular emotion? Sadness, anger, worry, fear, exhaustion, frustration and impatience are common habitual responses. What thoughts come into our mind? Themes of helplessness, victimization and unworthiness are familiar to many of us during times of stress. How do we experience our reactions physically? Do we experience emotional tension in our neck or shoulder muscles or is shortness of breath or a queasy stomach more familiar? Next, we must learn to recognize the stimuli. Which people or situations trigger our patterns of negative thoughts, emotions, and sensations?

The moment we become aware of a reaction, we alter the frequency of the reaction's vibrational wave to create an energetic space. This space allows us to shift our attention and take control of how we will respond. Awareness provides an opportunity to press the 'pause' button, attenuating the flood of neurotransmitters that initiate the cycle of heightened reactivity and reinforce our habitual responses. Awareness is not time dependent. It may come five minutes after an activating incident, five hours later, immediately after, or the next day. Regardless of the timing, awareness can help minimize the harmful consequences of our reactivity and strengthen our ability to react more constructively in the future.

With my patients, I often use the metaphor of a driver on a bus. The driver has an intended route and understands the importance of being aware of the passengers who may require help or pose potential challenges, especially those who often sit in the back and out of sight. To minimize the risk of anxious or angry passengers rushing forward to take control of the bus, the driver invites these passengers to sit up front where they can receive reassurance and attention. When we recognize our habitual patterns and their triggers, we can invite them to sit up front in our awareness, rather than in our unconscious mind, thus dissolving their skill in hijacking our emotional equilibrium. Awareness improves our ability to react from a calm and coherent state of mind rather than from our fear and anger, which compounds our suffering. The following narrative illustrates an application of the Heart-Mind Transformation Process. Jane is a pseudonym for one of my patients who used the steps to support her journey of transformation.

JANE

After many years of feeling overwhelmed, depressed, and angry regarding her twenty-four-year-old son's drug addiction, Jane decided to seek help. During our first session, Jane confided, "I feel so helpless." Pausing to wipe away tears and catch her breath, she continued, "I have tried to shut him out of my life, but that doesn't work either. I get so worried and then he calls, and I am sucked right back in, trying to help him. But then I just get so exhausted and frustrated." Holding space for her pain, I offered how this crisis could be a doorway to personal growth. When I showed her the hand model for the brain, opening up my fingers to indicate how fear-based emotions can 'flip our lids,' she smiled in recognition.

By understanding how the brain and body are hardwired for transformation as well as survival, Jane was able to view her story from an expanded perspective. She later shared that learning how emotional reactivity was a natural human struggle greatly relieved her despair and guilt. I helped her to develop awareness of where she experienced her reactivity in her body, teaching her to ride the waves of her emotions without feeling consumed by them. We discussed setting an intention to observe her thoughts, emotions and physical sensations without judgment. Two weeks later Jane reported having success. She shared that until now she had not felt connected to her body. She identified anger, sadness and guilt as her most common reactive emotions and discovered that shallow breathing and tightness in her chest often accompanied her reactivity.

Step 2: *B* = Breath

Many Eastern spiritual traditions promote the belief that *Breath* bears our universal life force energy, or *prana*. According to their teachings, working with our breath is the key to altering states of mind or effecting positive changes in the body. As the flow of breath conducts the flow of our energy, the flow of our energy shapes our state of mind. The simple act of breath awareness stimulates the region of our brain that creates coherent energetic resonance, the electromagnetic equivalent to feeling calm and peaceful.[67] Breath awareness also decreases neural firing in the brain stem, which helps us avoid flipping our lids. Research has discovered that experienced meditators take about half as many breaths per minute as those who do not meditate.[68] The slower and more deeply we breathe, the more peaceful we feel.

There are many different breathing practices that promote a sense of peace and clam. I have found the breath work described in Tenzin Wangyal Rinpoche's *Awakening the Sacred Bodies* highly effective.[69] Rinpoche provides a comprehensive guide to the nine breaths of purification, a Tibetan Bön practice of breath awareness and visualization that calms mind and body. My breath practice is a simplified version of the Bön nine breaths of purification, which I call the Calming Breath Practice.

Calming Breath Practice

Take three to five deep cleansing breaths. With each inhalation, visualize green light flowing into your lungs. With each exhalation, visualize yourself expelling a swirl of grey smoke. Connect to whatever comes into awareness. Now allow the content of that awareness (the thoughts, sensations, images, etc.) to dissolve into the exhalation of grey smoke. Recall a challenging habitual reaction. Allow the accompanying emotions, thoughts and physical sensations to emerge into your awareness. Now take three breaths. In the first breath, focus on your physical body, letting go of any tightness or tension along with the grey smoke. In

---

67 Siegel, D. Ibid. 2007.
68 Rama, Ballentine, & Hymes, *Science of Breath*. 2007.
69 Wangyal, T. Ibid. 2011.

the next breath, focus on your heightened emotions, calming and soothing them with a long, slow exhalation. In the third breath, attune to your thoughts, allowing their negativity to dissolve through another long, slow exhalation.

I suggest using this practice for five to ten minutes upon waking, another five to ten minutes during the middle of the day, and again before bedtime. You can progress to 15-20 minute sessions. The Calming Breath Practice can be used whenever you feel reactive or stressed. It can also be useful before engaging in a potentially triggering situation. When you feel ready, I recommend advancing to the Bön nine breaths of purification practice.

JANE

As Jane developed an increased awareness of her habitual reactions, she described feeling more spacious and centered. We then added breath work. Initially, Jane had difficulty breathing deeply and practicing long, slow exhalations as she was accustomed to shallow chest breathing. I recommended that she begin by only practicing deep inhalations and long slow exhalations several times a day or whenever she felt reactive or triggered. She soon advanced to the three breaths practice and found that attuning to her breath during times of irritation, such as standing in a slow grocery line or sitting in traffic, strengthened her ability to integrate breath work during highly stressful times.

Beginning with basic breathing exercises and then using my Calming Breath Practice, Jane had the confidence to move to the Bön nine breaths of purification practice. By applying breath awareness into her daily life Jane described feeling a sense of peace and calm and an improved capacity to cope with her emotional reactivity.

STEP 3: C = COMPASSIONATE WITNESS

After *Awareness* and *Breath*, the next step is to develop the *Compassionate Witness*. For most people practicing compassion is difficult. As with *Awareness*, self-acceptance and patience are crucial. Begin by attuning to your heart and then your breath. Visualize inhaling green light into your heart. When you exhale, release any negative emotions or dense energy. This creates energetic movement and space. Again visualize green light entering your heart as you inhale. Hold your breath and identify any dense, tight or frozen energy. As you exhale, again release the energy. Repeat three to five times.

As you release the dense energy, you may experience a sensation of warmth gathering in your heart or chest. Open yourself to compassion, filling your heart with gentleness and loving-kindness. Witness the emotions, thoughts or physical sensations that distress or challenge you. When you become distracted by your thoughts or environmental stimuli, acknowledge the distraction and gently return your attention to your breath and your heart. If you wish, you can add a mantra or soothing phrase. To do this, each time you inhale focus on your heart and say to yourself, "May I feel love (or compassion, peace, joy or whatever you chose)." When you exhale say, "May I release anxiety (or judgment, fear, anger, etc.)."

Sometimes highly charged or chaotic reactions will overwhelm your ability to invoke the compassionate witness. If this occurs, remind yourself that *feeling overwhelmed or out of control is part of the process*. Granting permission to struggle or regress is the work of the compassionate witness. Some habitual reactions feel so intractable that flipping our lids seems impossible to avoid. This is where we can incorporate other modalities to shift these stuck energy patterns. The field of Energy Psychology[70] provides effective strategies for short-circuiting deeply rooted conditioned responses.[71] Energy Psychology uses innovative tapping techniques on acupuncture points to shift frozen or stuck energy in our body and reprogram the brain's stress response.[72] As a diplomat certified energy psychology clinician, I have incorporated this simple, yet powerful transformative modality in my healing practice, and found that it can be easily taught to my patients.

---

70 www.energypsych.org
71 Gallo, F. *Energy Tapping for Trauma*, 2007.
72 Feinstein, D., Eden, D. & Craig, P. *The Promise of Energy Psychology*, 2005.

JANE

As Jane practiced self-acceptance and observed her reactions with loving kindness, she could begin to sit with her long-held emotional pain. The breath she brought into her heart soothed and loosened the dense energy of her disappointment and despair. Jane began to experience her compassionate witness as a wave of warm energy that cradled her pain and opened her heart. Along with the Bön nine breaths of purification she also incorporated energy psychology techniques into her daily practice. "My fogged-up mind seems clearer," she said. "I now see my torment through the eyes of a mother who watches her child suffer and can't do anything to help."

By observing her own habitual patterns with compassion, Jane could experience a new level of empathy for her son. Wisdom emerged where there had previously been judgment and fear. She could now understand that her son's drug addiction was a symptom of his own suffering. Jane could erect personal boundaries where none existed previously. "Compassion for my son is not the same as sadness. Something is different," she said. "I can feel his pain without getting sucked in." Jane's compassionate witness grew strong enough to cradle her own pain as well that of her son.

STEP 4: *D* = DESCRIBE AND DIALOGUE TO DIS-IDENTIFY AND DISSOLVE

Having practiced awareness, breathing and witnessing with compassion, we can move to the fourth and most complex of the Heart-Mind steps. The fourth step has two parts: *Describe* and *Dialogue*. When we describe or name our conditioned reactions, and then dialogue with the emotions, thoughts, sensations and images that emerge, we can learn to loosen and create more *Space*, and *Dis-identify* with habitual patterns and allow the charged energy to *Dissolve*. Our reactivity opens the portal to our shadow aspects.

Our shadow, while often frightening or disturbing, holds wisdom and power that can be accessed and integrated if we have the courage to acknowledge its existence and hear what it needs to say. The work of Step

4 allows us to invite the unclaimed aspects of ourselves into the light of awareness. This provides the needed *space* for us to release their hold on our reactivity and dissolve their destructive energy. Journaling can deepen the healing of this step. I highly recommend writing your descriptions and the content of your dialogue, as this provides more opportunity for insight and reflection. The ability to create more space is directly related to our wisdom view that we are not our emotions and beliefs, but within each of us is our true essence.

DESCRIBE

- Name the thought or emotion underlying your reaction.
- Describe the resulting sensation (e.g. warm, prickly, heavy, queasy, etc.) and location of where it resides in your body.
- Does the sensation have a color? If so, visualize the color. Sense its temperature and texture.
- Does your reaction evoke a shape or image? If so, describe it and its associated sensations.
- Does your reaction have a sound? If so, make the sound.
- Does your reaction have a taste or smell? If so, describe it.

Once you have compiled a thorough description of your reaction, return to steps A through C. Reconnect with your description, allowing the sensations, colors, images, and sounds to emerge into your awareness. Set an intention that this practice will promote a sense of calm and coherence. Focus on your breath. Is it more rapid or shallow than usual? Allow yourself to sense where the sensations or images reside in your body. Compassionately witness whatever arises. Do any of these sensations, colors, images, or sounds change? Note the changes and allow them to morph and shift, as they will. As we continue the practice, we will notice a *quickening*, whereby these steps appear to flow into one another and dis-identifying and dissolving becomes easier. When we are able to stabilize the unbalancing energetic waves of our reactions, we can increase our ability to rest in our true essence, which is boundless, unchanging and complete. Once we stabilize, we can deepen our wisdom and realizations.

STEVE

Another patient, Steve, uncovered a profound and healing insight using this practice. He first connected with his anger, which had been causing him and those close to him much distress. Steve described feeling a sensation of tightness in his shoulders and jaw. Almost immediately he saw the image of a dark wrathful figure. Without judging the image or succumbing to fear, he implemented steps A through C. Steve described what happened next as unexpected and unlike anything he had ever experienced. The dark figure transformed into a powerful and protective mother bear, a comforting image from his boyhood. Staring into the great beast's eyes, he penetrated her ferocity to reveal the love beneath her wrath. Steve knew in a flash that his anger had been shielding him from his own vulnerability. Instantly he felt his anger transmute into Mother Bear. By calling forth his anger, a frightening and powerful aspect of his shadow, and allowing it to reveal itself through Mother Bear, Steve reclaimed a fierce ally and protector. The next time he sensed the familiar tightening of his upper body, he could identify the emotion as vulnerability rather than anger, calling on Mother Bear to guide him in responding in a constructive, adaptive manner.

DIALOGUE

- Let go of any expectations, need to control, or rational thinking.
- Engage the emotion, image, sensation or sound, however your reactivity or shadow declared itself in the *Description* practice, by asking if it has a name. It can be a mythic name, or have a descriptive quality, like Mother Bear.
- Ask if it has an age or gender.

- What is its purpose?
- How long has it been waiting to be known to you?
- What does it want from you?
- What does it need from you?
- What is its message for you?

You can use two different methods for dialoguing with your reactivity. In the first method, you write your dialogue using different-colored pens, one color for you as the compassionate witness and another color for your reactivity voicing its message. The second method requires two chairs, one for the compassionate witness and one for your reactivity. You move from chair to chair embodying the different aspects of yourself. With either of these methods, remember to have patience and give each aspect the time and space to speak and reflect. Both methods are effective, so choose which one works best for you. My patients have found they prefer writing when working alone and using the chairs when in session with me.

As you continue to practice, you can return to a dialogue and start where you left off, as you would with an old friend. When finishing a dialogue, you can ask your reactivity or shadow where it would like to remain until it reveals itself again. Would it prefer to remain in front of you, on your lap, maybe along-side of you? If you ask, it will likely communicate its position.

Complete the dialogue by acknowledging the presence of your reactivity and expressing gratitude for its willingness to speak with you. Harness new information by regularly connecting with its energy and visualizing it in its chosen place. In this way, the incoherent energy of our reactivity becomes an external, rather than an internal part of you. This serves two purposes. First, you dis-identify with your habitual reaction, and second, its instinctual energy dissipates into the magnetic field beyond your body.

It is helpful to develop a relationship with your habitual reactions and reflect on what they want and need from you. Then you can go back to the first three steps: awareness, breath, and compassionate witness. By bringing compassion and opening your heart to different aspects of your reactivity, you can provide them with what they need and receive their power and their gifts.

STEVE

This excerpt of Steve's dialogue with Mother Bear illustrates how engaging our shadow can transform habitual reactions into powerful allies.

Steve: How long have you been with me?

Mother Bear: Since you were six. Do you remember when your father and older brother would hit you? You wouldn't get angry.

Steve: What do you want from me?

Mother Bear: I want you to see me. I get angry when you ignore me and forget what I have done for you. I am going to tear you to pieces. (She growls).

Steve: (Stunned and speechless) I am afraid of you. What do you need?

Mother Bear: Your appreciation!

Steve and Mother Bear continued this dialogue until Steve felt safer with the angry, demanding aspect of his shadow. He realized that his persistent rage possessed great power, a power he had feared throughout his life. During his Heart-Mind meditation practice, when he embodied the compassionate witness, Steve nurtured his anger by giving it the acknowledgment and the attention that it craved. Gradually Mother Bear metamorphosed into a luminous body in radiant pink and violet. Steve transformed his habitual anger into a steadfast capacity to protect and nurture.

STEP 5: *E* = EFFECTIVE AND EMPATHIC RESPONSE

The fifth step, *Effective* and *Empathic Response*, completes the Heart-Mind Process and is the fruit of utilizing steps A though D. When we do the work of the first four steps, our ability to respond effectively and empathically arises organically, allowing us to replace a habitual, conditioned reaction with one that is *calm* and *coherent*. An effective and empathic response eliminates the harm we cause others and ourselves by flipping our lids. There are times when the best response is no response. The Heart-Mind process provides us with the capacity to stop and wait before we act.

Return to Step 1 and practice awareness of any changes in how you respond to activating situations or people. What changes have you noticed in your emotions, thoughts or sensations? Have you become less reactive to certain triggers? How have your responses to stressful situations been more constructive? Which reactions have not changed? What are the obstacles to responding effectively, and how can the Heart-Mind Process help to dissolve those obstacles? You will know you have progressed to Step E if your responses:

- originate from a state of mind that is calm and coherent,
- express authentic thoughts and emotions,
- consider another's perspective, and
- convey respect and kindness

We must remember to celebrate the good work we have accomplished whenever we respond to activating experiences with calmness, authenticity, openness and kindness. Transforming our habitual patterns is a lifelong endeavor. The more we practice the more proficient we become.

JANE

After a few months of practicing the Heart-Mind Process, Jane experienced a softening in her heart and a stable, unflinching ability to sit with her pain. She experienced an inner spaciousness, in which she could witness her son's suffering without collapsing back to her habitual pattern of rescue and retreat. Having transformed her conditioned responses to her son's triggering behaviors, Jane felt ready to reach out to her son. They reconnected and this time their relationship was marked by clear boundaries. Jane knew how to be loving but firm. Most important, when Jane became aware of her sadness or guilt, her effective and empathic response was to open to her heart-mind and compassionately ride the waves of her challenging thoughts and emotions, dissolving the dense energy of her suffering. Although her son was still actively using drugs, Jane no longer felt trapped in a constant cycle of activation, reactivity, and suffering. Her journey became a testament to Rumi's wisdom that *"Grief can be the garden of compassion."* Jane's sadness, guilt, and despair took root and blossomed into a garden of compassion, the fruit of which became a faithful ally on her quest to an open heart.

REFLECTION

Become aware of your habitual patterns.
How do they manifest as thoughts, emotions and sensations?
Breathe into your open heart. Inhale green light.
Exhale grey smoke, allowing your reactive thoughts, emotions,
and sensations to dissolve through your exhalation.
Experience your dense, frozen energy loosening, softening, and dissolving.
Allow yourself to see through the eyes of the compassionate witness.
Fill your heart with self-acceptance, patience and loving kindness.
Surrender judgment and fear so that you may engage your shadow.
What does it want? What does it need? What are its gifts?
Acknowledge and celebrate your ability to respond to challenges
with a calm coherent state of mind and an open heart.

PART THREE
THE FRUITION

CHAPTER EIGHT
The Dance of Awareness

To see a world in a grain of sand
And a heaven in a wild flower,
Hold infinity in the palm of your hand
And eternity in an hour.

William Blake

Am I a man who dreamt of being a butterfly,
Or am I a butterfly dreaming that I am a man?

Chuang-Tzu

These words of William Blake and Chuang-Tzu reflect a consciousness much different from our daily waking perception. Their imagery transports us into a divine state of knowing that embraces the interconnectedness of all life and dissolves the barriers between spirit and the mundane. The word *consciousness* derives from the Latin word *conscius,* which has roots in the preposition *cum* meaning 'with' and the verb *scire,* 'to know.' Consciousness is a state of knowing that moves beyond cognitive understanding. It allows us to *know* with all avenues of our perception – cognitive, emotional, somatic, and spiritual.

Throughout the ages, poets, sages, philosophers and psychological theorists have recognized diverse levels of consciousness. Sanskrit has more than twenty terms for varied states of knowing. William James, the founder of Western psychology, believed that our waking consciousness exists along a continuum, and we must seek to experience the vast and varied levels available to us. James spoke of two ways of knowing: *conceptual* and *representative*.[73] Conceptual knowing is the most familiar, asserting our dualistic perception, in which the subject, the one who knows, is separate from the object, that which is known. Representative knowing, however, dissolves the separation between the knower and the known. For this we must embrace a non-dual notion of reality, unifying the one who experiences and the experience itself. In this oneness we dispel the illusion that we are separate from what is divine and whole, opening us to our own true nature, our divine essence.

Abraham Maslow, the humanist psychologist best known for his theory about the hierarchy of human needs, studied and documented consistent patterns of elevated consciousness. Maslow noted that the highest states possessed a mystical, spiritual quality in which we can experience unity, peace and wholeness. He termed these elevated states 'peak experiences.'[74] Philosopher Ken Wilber asserts that our peak experiences require cultivation and stabilization before they can bring about personal transformation. Wilbur sees our evolution from conditioned perceptions to spiritual awareness as an organic process comprised of various levels.[75] At each level, we must attain certain steps before advancing along the continuum. For Wilbur, availing ourselves of the integrative, healing power of higher consciousness requires diligence and practice.

Crisis can shatter our dualistic reality because who we think we are and what we think we know falls away. In the moment of collapse, we can cultivate methods to experience a unified awareness, an elevated state of consciousness that can introduce us to our pure and authentic selves. It is here, in this blissful state of knowing, that we find the true source of peace and wholeness.

---

[73] James, W. *The Varieties of Religious Experience*, 1902.
[74] Maslow, A. *Toward a Psychology of Being*, 1968.
[75] Wilber, K. *A Theory of Everything*, 2000.

PART THREE THE FRUITION

Returning to everyday awareness, we can shed the distorted belief that salvation is found by pursuing external sources of comfort and success.

Our path to awakening is a circuitous one, resembling a labyrinth rather than a straight line. To navigate and progress on the path we must satisfy developmental milestones. The first milestone requires that we recognize our habitual reactive patterns. From there, we must integrate the realization that the source of our reactivity arises from our conditioned identity rather than our authentic selves. With this insight we can move further into the heart of our journey and apply the Three Pillars of Transformation – compassionate awareness, listening with an open heart, and riding the waves of emotion – and the Heart-Mind process outlined in the previous chapters. We may feel awkward and shaky at first, taking missteps that lead us into confusion and uncertainty. Perseverance requires trust and faith. Once we believe we have the needed support and guidance to move along the path, we can begin the challenging and joyous journey back home to ourselves.

***

My journey of awakening freed me from the roles and expectations I assumed during my childhood. I could now see myself as an autonomous individual, connected to an inner source of wisdom and an infinite cosmic consciousness. Allied with faith in my intuitive knowing and belief in the mystical realm, I mustered the courage to journey deeper within, learning to recognize and integrate my own darkness. As I cultivated my compassionate witness and spent time listening to all that emerged from my mind and my heart, I felt myself expanding, becoming energetically lighter and more spacious. Studying Jung and working with Ann opened me to the realm of archetypes with its powerful symbols and images. Over time, divine states of knowing felt more real than my waking consciousness. My Buddhist meditation practices deepened my ability to remain mindful and dissolve my attachments to external ideas of comfort and success. Although I occasionally succumbed to my habitual reactions, by applying the Three Pillars and Heart-Mind process these moments of reactivity became less amplified and my ability to access cosmic consciousness strengthened. I was learning to cultivate and stabilize these cosmic encounters. I found myself moving along the spectrum of consciousness and spent more time at the levels Wilbur termed *self-transcendence* and *psychic unity.*

Like Jung, who felt the presence of spiritual beings, I too began to experience the presence of numinous energy, especially Kuan Yin, who first came to me while at Esalen. Experiencing Kuan Yin deepened my ability to become a compassionate witness, and my work as a therapist began to shift. As my patients recounted their suffering, I could glimpse fleeting scenes and images surrounding them. My body became an antenna that could sense their psychic pain and the location of their frozen energy. Initially, I felt surprised and bewildered. Fortunately, I was still working with Linda, my guide, as I opened to cosmic consciousness. She reassured me that my newfound ability was indeed a *siddhi*, a gift of my awakening. She called my gift *clairsentience,* the ability to sense and experience others' emotional and physical energy.

Through Linda I came to learn of other *siddhis* that can accompany higher states of consciousness, including levitation and astral projection. The Dalai Lama describes expert spiritual practitioners as developing "meditative concentration to the point of becoming clairvoyant and generating miracles."[76] Milarepa, a thirteenth-century Tibetan yogi, was said to possess the power to levitate. Western mystical traditions also recognize *siddhis*. As a young child, Saint Hildegard of Bingen told of entering radiant, spiritual states accompanied by fantastical visions. Witnesses reported seeing Saint Teresa of Avila levitate during a state of rapture. While *siddhis* are not the goal of cultivating spiritual consciousness, they can arise as a result of practices that expand our notion of reality. Linda cautioned that the moment we grasp or attach to *siddhis*, they will be lost.

With one foot firmly planted in the visible realm of daily existence, I stepped with the other into a pervasive and invisible field of awareness. My outer reality reflected the expansiveness of my inner journey. I began receiving

---

76 Dalai Lama. *Becoming Enlightened*, 2009, p.88.

PART THREE THE FRUITION

invitations to present at conferences, often sponsored by women's organizations. Feeling silenced for most of my life, I was filled with a sense of power and purpose when I was elected president of the National Organization for Chinese American Women in Los Angeles. My children accompanied me to rallies, toy drives, and holiday events for families in need. I wanted Randy and Jennifer to experience our shared human connection and the gifts of community and volunteerism. I cared little for the empty ideals of achieving straight A's or fulfilling conventional definitions of success. For Randy and Jennifer I wanted lives filled with connection, compassion, and awakening.

During this time I continued meditating and entering into the mystical realm. While watching the news one evening, the story of an apprehended serial killer caught my attention. As the suspect's face flashed on the screen, I was overcome with hatred and an instinctual need to destroy. I knew this violent emotion was at first the suspect's, and then my own terrifying repulsion. The intensity of my emotions shocked and frightened me. Gradually, as my breathing steadied, I entered a field of golden light. All at once the light dispelled the dark and violent energy, transforming the hatred and repulsion into compassion and bathing the suspect's image with light. Only a minute or two had passed, but the time felt much longer. I had touched a mystery, feeling the suffering of those for whom we spare little compassion.

For the next few months, I continued cultivating and stabilizing my experiences of psychic unity. I found myself becoming one with everyday objects such as stones and trees. As expected, I felt drawn to the pleasant and positive experiences and avoided the challenging ones. I was aware of my inclinations and aversions and even detected moments of pride related to my emerging gifts, reminding myself not to submit to arrogance or self-importance. My meditation practice now focused on my habitual reactions, which I knew obscured my connection to the divine.

Like Mother Teresa, my darkness was a coveted doorway to evolving consciousness. The poetry of the Vietnamese monk, Thich Nhat Hahn, reflected my experience. "I am the child in Uganda, all skin and bones, my legs as thin as bamboo sticks, and I am the arms merchant, selling deadly weapons to Uganda."[77] I understood that opening to the divine meant embracing my inner demons, so that no separation existed between the light and the dark. The depth of this truth filled my heart with boundless love as I continued to navigate the realms of awareness.

***

Although seeking the mystical realm can leave us unbalanced and confused at times, recognizing the guidance of dreams and synchronicities can provide valuable encouragement. A few years after my awakening, a brochure arrived in the mail advertising a three-week seminar at the Jung Institute in Switzerland. Instantly captivated, a lack of ready cash tempered my enthusiasm. A persistent inner voice, however, dismissed money as a trifling excuse. I decided to register. The day after mailing the application, I received a statement from a German bank showing I had an existing balance. I laughed when seeing the amount – just enough to cover my expenses. Soon after, a dear friend called in need of a place to stay. Her timing coincided with my seminar. She was happy to look after the children whom she knew so well. These *co-incidences* recalled earlier windfalls – my free session with Linda and the lottery ticket that financed a year's worth of sessions with her. Once again I found obstacles being cleared by an unseen hand.

Shortly before leaving for Switzerland, I had a telling dream. Dressed like Alice in Wonderland, I found myself standing at a crossroads, pondering two directions. Suddenly, a spiraling image appeared on my hand urging me leftward. Two steps into my journey the ground fell away, hurtling me into a dark void. I felt strangely calm as I surrendered to a great cosmic force. I awoke elated, the spiral symbol still visible on my left hand. Meditating on the dream's meaning, I viewed the spiral as a symbol of rebirth and the feminine, receptive aspect of myself.

---

77 Hahn, Thich Nhat. *Peace is Every Step*, 1992.

PART THREE THE FRUITION

Through my spiritual studies, I had come to learn about the archetypal principle of the divine feminine. In all mystical traditions, there exists an infinite source of unity and wholeness, a Oneness from which emerges the vibration of opposing forces – the feminine and masculine, the yin and yang, the being and the doing. These pairs of opposites are qualities that exist within each of us, irrespective of our sex or gender. Masculine qualities relate to action, manifestation and mastering the physical world. They include the ideals of analytical thought, evidence-based information, conquest, competition, and authority. Feminine qualities, however, relate to stillness, receptivity and communion with the physical and unseen worlds. They include intuition, wisdom, emotion, collaboration and cooperation. For centuries, masculine attributes have dominated Western and Eastern cultures, maligning and negating feminine qualities. Without the balancing influence of the feminine, however, masculine archetypal energy has grown distorted and dangerous, fostering a world culture of aggression, acquisition, and exploitation. Marion Woodman, a Jungian analyst and scholar of the sacred feminine, describes feminine consciousness as "feelings, needs, and values, and has the courage to act on them." Woodman portrays someone with feminine wisdom as one who "understands resonance – truth resonating in her body, like an echo chamber saying, 'Yes.' She is a receiver."[78] Feminine wisdom holds the human form and the earth itself as sacred, not objects for exploitation. And like the natural cycle of the seasons, it adheres to the pervasive mystical belief that life is a cycle of beginnings and endings, the truth that without death there is no rebirth.

Like Alice's fall down the rabbit hole, the never-ending cycle of death and rebirth was a central motif in my Wonderland dream. I shared this dream with Ann, who recalled two well-known myths that illuminate the mystery of the divine feminine. The first was the Greek tale of Persephone, the archetypal daughter who, while distractedly gathering flowers in a springtime meadow was abducted by Hades, King of the Underworld. Desperate and grief stricken, Persephone's mother Demeter, goddess of the harvest, sought intervention

---

78 Woodman, M. *Conscious Femininity*, 1993, p.86.

from Zeus, who finally relented and presented an offer Hades couldn't refuse. With this agreement, Persephone was released from her captivity in darkness. Persephone emerged a queen, dividing her time between reigning in the Underworld, our autumn and winter, and returning above ground six months later, our spring and summer.[79] Like Persephone, my descent was a preparation for owning my own sacred feminine nature, allowing my young maiden to die, so I could return as the queen, navigating the visible and invisible realms, the darkness along with the light. The second myth was the Descent of Inanna. In the ancient Sumerian story, Inanna, the goddess of heaven travels to the Underworld in search of her sister. Her journey into the realm of darkness reflects our own need to face and integrate the shadow so we may return to wholeness, the archetypal Self.[80]

My dream of descent became a powerful ally while preparing for the three-week conference. Guilt about leaving the children raised doubts about my decision. However, the dream dispelled my uncertainties and reinforced my connection with the sacred feminine. Books and study alone would not satisfy my longing to learn more about the divine feminine principles of death and rebirth, of claiming the power of our own darkness for integration and wholeness. I knew I needed to pursue my own transformational journey, leaving behind what was known and familiar, just like my dream, just like Persephone and Inanna.

This trip would be my first to Europe since leaving Germany in 1984. The long flight to Zurich provided me time to reflect on how I had changed during the past four years. I left Europe as a timid, voiceless young woman, who was battling bulimia and depression. And now I was returning, like a phoenix from the ashes – a confident, bold woman, initiated into the power and mysteries of the invisible realm.

The Jung Institute was a simple, elegant two-story house on the shores of a tranquil lake. Surrounding the house was a well-maintained garden, dotted with benches facing the water. Despite the unforgiving wind blowing off the

---

[79] Shinoda Bolen *The Goddesses in Every Woman*, 1984.
[80] Perera S. *Descent to the Goddess*, 1981.

PART THREE THE FRUITION

lake, I treasured my long afternoon walks in the bracing air. I felt open and free with no need to plan or organize. Without conscious thought or effort I embraced the divine feminine principle of simply being and remaining open to any experience that came my way. On a scheduled day off from the seminar, I took a train to nearby Bollingen, Jung's home. I wanted to experience the place where my teacher had intuited the collective unconscious, wrestled with his shadow, and wrote his many works. Standing by the gate in the pouring rain, I peered into the garden and felt Jung's presence. After my pilgrimage, I took refuge at a nearby inn, easing my chill with a glass of mulled wine. Sipping my drink and ruminating on the events of the day, I found myself transfixed by the tales of an elderly local, who claimed to be a former resident of Bollingen. The old man regaled me with stories of the house, Jung himself, and the luminaries who came to visit. We both traveled back in time that day, caught up in the numinous magic of recollected memories on a rainy afternoon.

The conference was nearing its end. Distanced from my routine, immersed in the peace of being and allowing, I honed my subtle hearing and perception. During a mid-afternoon break, I retreated to the basement tearoom. Sinking into a comfortable sofa, I closed my eyes and inhaled the musty air. All at once I felt myself transported to the realm of spacious cosmic consciousness. Overcome by a pervasive sorrow, images emerged of women enduring the ancient Chinese tradition of foot binding, a perverted symbol of female beauty and desirability. Amid agonizing screams and protests, I watched as their feet were systematically broken, bent and tightly bound into a ball. I felt their excruciating pain turn to numbness and then resignation.

The images were replaced with sounds. A faraway voice whispered, "Unbinding the soul." Immediately, I knew this was to be the title of my own story. The barbarity of foot binding had long been abolished in China. Yet I, like so many others before me, was bent, broken, and bound by conditioned traditional roles and expectations. Through my crisis and awakening I freed myself from the trappings of my external identity. There in the basement of the Jung

Institute, I descended into the abyss of my unconscious and claimed a powerful message – that I was to write and share my journey of transformation.

Like Persephone and Inanna, I had survived a cycle of death and rebirth. Dutiful Barbara had died in the underworld that was my crisis. I reemerged reborn, connected to cosmic consciousness, unbound from others' needs and expectations, and ready to claim what was authentic and true. I returned to Los Angeles with a new and intimate knowledge of my divine feminine nature. I could recognize in myself the words of Marion Woodman. Now aware of my own feelings, needs, and values, my journey to Switzerland expressed the courage to act on my inner knowing. The descent motif of my initiatory dream had manifested in the gifting of the title for this book, which arose from the stillness of the invisible realm. I was now ready to embody the sacred feminine and fulfill the message that said I was to share my journey of healing and awakening.

BEACON OF THE SACRED FEMININE

The magic of my encounter in the basement of the Jung Institute continued when I returned home. The seed of *Unbinding the Soul* took root and numinous images and sounds continued to grow more vivid and astounding. My homecoming was blessed with a dreamtime visitation from the divine feminine. A beautiful woman bathed in golden light appeared and extended her arms to me. I responded, allowing her to pull me close and cloak me in the purity and strength of her love. In the days that followed I nurtured an intimacy with my sacred vision, entreating her to appear and engaging her in dialogue. "I am the Mother of the Universe," she said. "I have been your guide for many lifetimes. Remember when you sat on the rooftop as a girl listening to the wind and gazing at the sky? You heard me then and I ask you to hear me now. You are to become a beacon for the sacred feminine."

Hearing these words spoken through the vibration of infinite love, I shed tears of joyful recognition, reclaiming the little girl who danced on the Hong Kong rooftop. With each breath I cleared my dense energy, opening myself to become a vessel of the divine feminine, ready to receive and share her wisdom and her blessings. My life continued as a dance between the two distinct yet interwoven worlds of body and spirit. At times the stress of my waking life would prevail, filling me with doubt and disrupting my mystical connection. Questions such as "How can I take on more responsibility?" and "What if I fail?" remained at the periphery of my awareness ready to distract and confound. Yet these moments strengthened my resolve and provided opportunities to practice the Heart-Mind process. I found myself recognizing, listening to and riding the waves of the emotions and experiences that came my way, deepening my ability to receive, surrender and trust. Externally, I sought signs to guide me to a teacher. I took classes taught by gifted healers, but none of their traditions called to me. Meanwhile, my primary teacher was Kuan Yin, the essence of the divine feminine, the manifestation of the Mother of the Universe, who cradled me and nourished me with her wisdom of love and compassion.

Parenting, work, and community involvement remained my focus. Yet, the book and the message from my dream maintained a hold on my psyche. When I finished my term as president of the Organization of Chinese American Women, the opportunity to attend a writing class at Esalen presented itself. The time had come to begin writing. Despite my enthusiasm, progress was slow. Two years passed before I wrote the first sentence. Documenting my personal journey of awakening took another three years. Although my writing came in fits and starts, the process proved inspiring and healing.

On occasion I would share my writing with my mother, who greatly appreciated this new intimacy. As a devout Catholic, my mother possessed a faith that was pure and encompassing. Though our views about religion differed, we shared a deep affection for Our Lady of Guadalupe and Mother Mary, Christian embodiments of the sacred feminine. Through shared conversations and witnessing my inner growth, my mother learned to honor her own feminine strength and wisdom. After seven decades, my mother found the courage to disclose the truth of her incest to her sisters. She later revealed, "I feel so much freer now. I know that I need to forgive my father, and your father too. Thank you for sharing and listening." In healing myself, my mother too could become whole, finding new sources of courage in my reflected strength.

INITIATION INTO THE SHAMANIC PATH

As I continued to cultivate and stabilize my cosmic encounters, two dreams propelled me into the next phase of my journey. The first dream was short but profound. There was no image, just an insistent voice. "Do you not know that you are on the shaman's path?" The voice felt more declarative than interrogative. Despite the force behind the message, I resisted the call. For years my goal was to be a Jungian analyst, a title my conditioned identity considered more acceptable than a shaman. A few weeks later I had a second dream, amplifying the message of the first. In the dream, I observed an unidentifiable force severing my limbs and rearranging them neatly into a mandala. I knew that my life would take an unexpected turn.

I shared my dream with Ann, who went to her shelf, took down a book, and opened to a page with a photo of the mandala I had described. The book was by Mircea Eliade, an anthropologist who documented symbolic dismemberment initiations in shamanic cultures.[81] Eliade described how, as part of a shaman's apprenticeship, the initiate falls ill and experiences a vision of dismemberment and reconstitution. Jung too wrote of this initiation. "The dismemberment motif belongs in the wider context of rebirth symbolism. Consequently it plays an important part in the initiation experiences of shamans . . . who are dismembered and put together again."[82] Reading this quote aloud, Ann looked at me and said, "You might wish to listen to what the spirits are telling you."

Stunned by the parallel between my dream imagery and those found in the shamanic rites of other cultures, I knew I could no longer dismiss shamanism as a primitive superstition. With Ann's encouragement, I hesitantly started

---

81 Eliade, M. *Shamanism: Archaic Techniques of Ecstasy*, 1964.
82 *Collected Works of C.G. Jung*, 1961, 11, p.346.

reading about shamanism. Once again I found myself engaged in the energetic web of cosmic connection. It was time to heed the call.

***

Shamanism is an ancient healing tradition found predominantly in indigenous cultures throughout the world, including Siberia, Africa, Europe, Australia, and the Americas. Shamanic traditions believe that all life is infused with an energy that originates from an invisible spirit world. The word 'shaman' derives from *samon,* used by the Evenki people of Siberia to designate a priest of their religion. *Shaman* has been variously translated as 'one who sees in the dark,' 'one who knows' or 'healer.' Another definition describes a shaman as 'one who knows ecstasy,' implying the connection with the spirit realm can bring about a rapturous experience. A shaman has the ability to transcend the normal limits of consciousness. She or he intercedes for people by traveling to the upper and lower spirit worlds for the purposes of healing, reclaiming life energy, removing negative forces, and bringing back messages from the void. Shamans value a harmonious relationship between nature and humanity and serve to repair and cultivate this relationship for the purposes of healing and transformation.

Within shamanic traditions there exist varying levels practice. While most shamans focus on healing physical and spiritual imbalances, some co-op their gifts to attain power, harm others or control enemies. The highest level of shamanism seeks to manifest personal integration and wholeness for the benefit of all beings. This level, which I term Mystic Shamanism, represents a bridge between the Source and all beings. The mystic shaman cultivates and experiences the divine through deep meditation and prayer as well as through everyday encounters. Their capacity to connect with the energy of the Source, both in the spirit realm and within themselves gives mystic shamans astonishing healing powers.

The call to shamanism occurs in varying ways. Some are anointed at birth. Some receive a direct transmission from an elder within an established lineage, and others may be called during a personal vision or dream, often following a personal crisis. My call to shamanism came in a series of dreams. For years I had immersed myself in the works of Jung. Through my ongoing spiritual studies I came to view my mentor as a modern shaman, his theories strikingly similar to many shamanic beliefs. I believed that Jung himself had opened a door. I knew I must step through it and venture further.

***

Dreams continued to guide me on my shamanic path. The next instructive dream found me dancing on a stage with Jesus. A cobra appeared, hissing violently. Strangely, I was not afraid. I began to move with the cobra, holding its penetrating gaze. The creature became mesmerized. I reached out, but before I could take hold of its throat, I awoke. Again, I shared my dream with Ann. She agreed with my intuition that my psyche was prompting me to make a connection between Christ consciousness and the Kundalini energy of Eastern mysticism. Despite Ann's validation, I remained uncertain of the dream's relevance. A few weeks later a synchronistic event revealed more of its message.

I was watching a television documentary on indigenous culture and healing. The film showed a Balinese shaman walking up a mountain, as part of an initiation ritual. She reached a cave in which a cobra lay coiled. The shaman began to move in an unusual way, making strange sounds and enticing the cobra to rise. As the shaman swayed, her eyes fixed on those of the cobra. Suddenly, the snake grew still. The shaman leaned forward and kissed the flat part of the cobra's nose and then quietly and calmly retreated from the cave. Astounded by this image, I realized that my dream was asking me to deepen my shamanic path, and that Bali was the next leg of my journey.

Trusting in the ways of spirit, I decided to search for a Balinese shaman in my area. I also began studying Balinese culture. Yet no other signs appeared. I continued my meditation practice and focused on my daily life. Months later, while attending a meditation retreat in northern California, I came across a flyer announcing, 'Yoga retreat in the magical land of Bali.' By letting go of my expectations and dissolving my excitement about the similarity between my dream and the documentary, I had arrived at a place of receptivity. A few weeks later, I was in Bali. The moment I stepped onto to the island, I could feel the presence of spirits. Shrines graced every doorway, and the Balinese prayed and made offerings each morning. Rituals continued throughout the day. This pilgrimage, like Switzerland before, would reveal new portals into the mystical realm.

The retreat began each day with yoga, followed by visits to temples and meetings with shamanic healers. During breaks, I took long walks and enjoyed relaxing massages. As I soaked in a pool of fragrant water, covered with petals of flowers, I gave thanks to the Divine. It had been almost a decade since my crisis, and so much had changed. I knew there were no certainties. I knew these blessings could vanish in a moment. But I felt certain of one thing: I could trust my inner knowing. I had come to Bali to receive, to be a vessel of the sacred feminine.

My faith was rewarded on our first outing. My group traveled to Mount Agung, Bali's most famous mountain and the highest peak on the island. Tradition holds that Mount Agung is a replica of Mount Meru, the mystical mountain of Tibet, and the central axis of the universe. Meditating on the temple grounds, I entered the spirit world with ease. Overcome with bliss, I was instantly transported to the realm of the Great Mother of the Universe, who manifested as two female figures. Kuan Yin appeared on my left and the Mother Mary on my right. "We are the Eastern and Western Mothers of the Universe," they declared. "You are to be a beacon for us, and to unify the different traditions. There is but one Source." They held me in their radiant loving energy, filling my heart with a powerful light. Kuan Yin and Mother Mary then shared a message for another member of our group. "Please tell her that she will be a wonderful mother."

For a long time, I remained still, held in Great Mother's loving embrace. Fortunately, the group leader understood that I was experiencing a moment of *satori*, or oneness, and left me to meditate in the beauty of a sacred garden. The leader continued guiding the others through the temple grounds. When I emerged from my encounter, filled with the blessing of the sacred feminine, the group had returned. I approached the woman for whom I had received Great Mother's message. "This might sound strange," I said with some hesitation, "But I was given the message that you will be a wonderful mother." The woman first stared, and then broke into an unforgettable smile. She shared that she had come to Bali because she was at a crossroads in her life. She was nearing the end of her child bearing years and married to a wonderful man who was eager to be a father. Her obstacle was a deep fear. "My mother had been so terrible to me," she said, "I feel I might be too damaged to be a mother." While touring the temple she had been praying for an answer to her dilemma. "Your message has been a tremendous gift."

During the next two weeks, I was gifted with more visions and messages. Despite my excitement, I remained connected to the wisdom of humility and nonattachment. My time in Bali deepened my shamanic gifts, but also exposed me to a darker side of shamanism. I felt myself excited by some shamans who demonstrated their extraordinary power. Transfixed by the magic I witnessed, I could feel myself intoxicated and drawn to give away my authority, similar to the seductive force of the Ring in Tolkien's fictional work. Fortunately, I felt the presence of the Great Mother, who woke me up with a piercing sound. At that moment of recognition, I 'saw' filaments of vibration being sucked by these shamans from the bodies of patients they were treating. Instead of being horrified and repulsed, my heart opened and the compassionate wisdom flowed from my heart to embrace these dark facets of humanity. Returning to Los Angeles, I ceased my childlike romanticizing of exotic cultures, shamans and mystics. I learned the invaluable lesson that even mystical power can seduce and corrupt. Most importantly, though, my Balinese pilgrimage allowed me to receive the healing power of compassionate resonance, to become an echo chamber of the universe, and answer 'yes' to the call to be a mystic shaman healer.

PART THREE THE FRUITION

BECOMING THE RAVEN

While on my search for a spiritual teacher I was asked to become one instead. A dear friend of mine, Meida, who was a Buddhist and Chinese medicine practitioner, invited me to her center in Asia to lead a workshop on mind and body healing. En route to Taiwan, I stopped in Hong Kong to visit my father. I had not returned to my childhood home since Gary's death. Aware of my father's dissolute lifestyle I chose to stay with friends. Yet nothing prepared me for the state in which I found his apartment. Tenants occupied most of the rooms, including the garage. My father's quarters held our old furnishings, which were thick with dust. Family photos, including my parents' wedding photo, held pride of place on the coffee table. I felt a growing sadness and a yearning to rescue my father from his lonely existence.

Aware of my heavy emotions and the constriction around my heart, I created healing space by breathing into my chest. Waiting for the waves of emotion to subside, I noticed a Buddhist shrine in the dining area. My father had returned to his family's spiritual lineage. In this, we shared a unifying bond. "Dad," I asked spontaneously, "Have you been to the monastery on Lantau Island?" His eyes lit up at my invitation to visit the largest Buddhist statue in Asia. After a long boat ride, we found the temple grounds crowded with tourists and pilgrims. I held my father's hand as we climbed the steep stairs to the entrance. We entered the temple in silence. We each lit a stick of holy incense. Together we bowed to the deities of our ancestors.

My father looked up, unable to express the depth of his emotion. I began to discern images dancing in the light about his head – my father as a boy, running around our ancestral home in the Szechuan countryside; my grandmother, a devout Buddhist, lighting incense and teaching her young son to bow. The moment was fleeting. An ambling tourist accidentally knocked into my father, igniting his still short fuse. We ferried back to Hong Kong and parted with a goodbye hug. This was the last time I would see my father before we again shared prayers at his deathbed.

***

After returning from Asia, I came across a brochure for a training program in Heart-Centered Clinical Hypnotherapy.[83] Trusting my inner knowing, I registered for the six-day course. On day one we learned to enter trance. Almost in the first moment of the first exercise I started to shiver, my teeth chattering uncontrollably. Two fellow participants covered me with blankets, but my reaction only intensified. Panicked, my would-be helpers sought the support of the instructor who immediately took charge.

"Where are you?" the instructor asked. Still in trance, I took in my surroundings, realizing I was a tiny infant covered in snow. This was my first journey to a past life. The story of this baby girl unfolded quickly. I was in Afghanistan, about a hundred-fifty years ago. My peasant farmer parents lacked the resources to care for me. My desperate father carried me beyond the village where I could die unseen and unknown. My chest seized as the frigid air filled my lungs. Unable to breathe, I lost consciousness and soon died. I woke from the trance. Under the instructor's deft guidance, I integrated the unresolved lesson from that lifetime of being unworthy and a burden as a girl child. Reclaiming what felt like a piece of my soul, this past-life encounter shifted something deep within me. Yearning to learn more, I registered for two additional years of intensive instruction. My hypnotherapy training would introduce me to a murder of ravens and my first encounter with a raven spirit.

The advanced instruction focused on entering and managing trance states, followed by a one-year internship. Trainings were held outside Seattle and organized into two annual five-day retreats. During the second retreat, on a gloomy November morning, a gathering of majestic jet-black birds claimed my attention with their imperious cawing and graceful swooping and soaring. Although I knew little of ravens prior to the training, my exposure to the totemic traditions of the Northwest taught me that these intelligent birds are

---

83 Wellness Institute has one of the most comprehensive hypnotherapy-training programs in the United States.

PART THREE THE FRUITION

the *messengers from the void,* traveling into the unseen realms, returning with messages and healing power.

During the retreat, raven images repeatedly appeared in Tarot card readings and in dreams. Yet it was not until the final day of training that my personal relationship with the raven spirit was revealed. While practicing breath work, I suddenly became racked with pain, feeling an unseen force twist and elongate my limbs. My nose and jaw contorted into a beak-like shape, and wings sprouted from my back. I felt myself shape-shift into an enormous raven. My metamorphosis complete, I flew off to explore faraway planets and stars, soaring for what felt like hours before morphing back into my physical form. Awaking from the trance, a voice declared, "You are to take on the raven's name and spirit." My fellow participants looked awestruck, unanimously describing a radiant energy emanating from my body throughout the exercise.

Seven years passed before accepting the mantle of the raven spirit and legally changing my name from Barbara to Raven. During that time, I danced with the raven energy and strengthened my ability to travel to different realms. As the relationship with cosmic consciousness is ever evolving, I continued to cultivate my connection with the raven for many years. When doubts arose, I would bring them into awareness, invoking my compassionate witness and sitting with trust and patience until the right action became known. Much time passed before I truly embodied the raven, becoming a *messenger from the void,* returning with messages and healing power of the divine feminine. My human struggles continued to arise, a reminder that the ebb and flow of reactive emotions are lifelong companions.

Another formative crisis occurred a year following my raven initiation. My son, Randy, home from college for Thanksgiving, had fallen asleep on the couch after too much turkey and stuffing. While washing dishes, I heard a thud. I rushed into the living room to find Randy writhing on the floor, seizing uncontrollably. Instinctively, I put my finger in his mouth (which I later learned was dangerously incorrect) and waited in dread for the paramedics to arrive.

I could hear the clamor of my heart and feel fear congealing in my throat and chest. Gazing at Randy, I found myself in the midst of a distant memory. Sitting in the front seat of my car, I had turned to check on my infant son, who inexplicably began to convulse. The memory appeared as an undeveloped photo that finally came into focus. Cradling my twenty year old, I was also holding my toddler. Images of other incidents emerged – Gary berating or hitting a confused little boy while I stood by, powerless to intervene. In the five minutes before the ambulance arrived I had journeyed back to past wounds of helplessness, bearing witness to my own suffering and that of my son. I became the raven who could travel into the void to retrieve distant wounds, bringing them into the light of awareness.

The wail of the siren instantly returned me to my present horror. Randy was stabilized and rushed to the hospital where he was swallowed into the cold glare beyond my reach. The night was a desperate wait as Randy underwent numerous blood draws, electrographs and imaging. Once again my fear froze in my chest. In the early hours of the morning the neurologist delivered the news that Randy had a small tumor in his brain. There was no treatment. Time alone would reveal if the mass would grow.

Unlike my crisis after Gary's death, I now had the guidance of Kuan Yin and my raven spirit. Rather than fight against my fear and sadness, I held them in a compassionate embrace, surrendering to my vulnerability, allowing my heart to render in two. I accepted my impotence, dissolving the illusion of the all-protecting mother, acknowledging the horrible truth that my children could die. I realized how much effort I had wasted worrying. Knowing the devastation caused by their father's death, I feared that Randy and Jennifer could also succumb to depression or suicide. Now, however, I let go of my hopes and expectations around Randy's diagnosis, trusting that, whatever the outcome, we could learn and grow together.

During that time, I prayed, meditated, grieved, and sent healing energy to Randy, who retreated into solitude. I had to respect my son's way of coping with his pain. As the raven, I traveled to the void, gaining strength as I deepened my wisdom of death and rebirth. During one journey, I received a clear message that I must honor Randy's initiation and trust in its unique unfolding. There were moments when I danced as the raven, unfettered by human worries, and moments when I embodied the powerless mother, riding waves of anguish and despair, keening and weeping at the possibility of losing my son. Each time I surfaced from the cloying pain, I gained strength in my belief that beneath the pain lay a vast ocean of calm and faith.

We arrived at the six-month checkup filled with trepidation. I took steady, deep breaths and chanted a silent prayer in preparation for hearing the latest imaging results. "The tumor is gone," the neurologist declared with an equal measure of calm and certainty. Gratitude swept through me like a cleansing wind. Although a parent's worst fear was not realized, the experience reinforced the invaluable lessons of mortality, impermanence and trust. I recognized that the next challenge on my spiritual quest would be to move beyond fear and hope.

REFLECTION

When did you last experience a moment of bliss, peace or wholeness?
Return to the experience.
What were your thoughts, emotions, and sensations?
Have you ever felt supported or guided by an unseen force or presence?
Return to the experience.
What were your thoughts, emotions, and sensations?
Do you have a siddhi, a gift of awakening, a realization?
If so, name it.
Return to the time your siddhi first declared itself to you.
What were your thoughts, emotions, and sensations?
When have you had a dream that upon waking felt like a message?
Did the message guide you in your waking life?
How often do you experience coincidences or synchronicities?
Do they feel random or do they have meaning for you?
When have you ventured beyond what is known and safe?
What did you discover about yourself?
When have you allowed your heart to break fully and completely open?
What did you discover about yourself?

CHAPTER NINE
Beyond Hope and Fear

I said to my soul, be still, and wait without hope.
For hope would be hope for the wrong thing: wait without love.
For love would be love of the wrong thing: there is yet faith.
But the faith and love and the hope are all in the waiting.
Wait without thought, for you are not ready for thought:
So the darkness shall be the light, and the stillness the dancing.

T. S. Eliot

Self-arising wisdom is the base.
The five negative emotions are manifested energy.
Seeing emotions as mistaken is an error.
Letting them be in their nature is the method
to find the non-dual state of Liberation.
Overcoming hope and fear is the result.

Tenzin Wangyal Rinpoche

Long ago, in a remote province of China, there lived an old man with his only son. The man had but one prized possession, a fine black stallion and the envy of his fellow villagers. One day, the horse succeeded in breaking free from his rickety coral. News spread swiftly and the villagers came running to offer their condolences. "What a misfortune!" they lamented, feigned regret audible to the old man's ears. The old man smiled a wise old smile and replied, "Perhaps." A few weeks later, the stallion returned to his coral, bringing with him a herd of exquisite wild horses. News spread swiftly and the villagers came running to offer their congratulations. "What good fortune is this!" they exclaimed, envy audible to the old man's ears. The old man smiled a wise old smile and replied, "Perhaps."

Perplexed by their neighbor's lack of exuberance, the villagers retreated, shaking their heads. The next day, while breaking a wild horse, the old man's son shattered his thighbone. Once again, the villagers gathered, this time to sympathize. "What a tragedy!" they gasped. "Your dear son will be crippled for life." The old man's heart warmed at his neighbors' genuine concern. The old man smiled his wise old smile and replied, "Perhaps." This time the villagers felt certain the old man had lost his mind. Days after, a local overlord declared war on a nearby province, conscripting all young men of the village, save the old man's son who was crippled. The young men marched off to battle. They would never return.

The wise old man's circumstances show us the futility of fearing tragedy and hoping for good fortune. No matter the circumstance, the wise old man remained content and at peace knowing that the wheel of fortune circles ever thus. As a child living in a chaotic household, I wanted to be the old man who could remain calm and unafraid despite his ordeals. But I understood the villagers too. Why not be devastated when faced with tragedy? Why not feel elation when good luck came my way? I could not penetrate the wisdom that cloaked the old man in his peace and contentment. To defend against my constant anxiety, I clung to the hope that when I grew up, unlike my mother, I would have a loving and loyal husband who made me feel safe. No matter how dark my present, my hope for a happier future kept me going.

As my journey of awakening unfolded, I had much to learn before I could trade my fear and hope for the old man's equanimity. While I grew more adept at traversing the mystical realm and shedding the illusions that veiled my true nature, I held fast to the misguided notion that moving toward wholeness could brake fortune's wheel before it made its downward turn. Not until I learned the lesson of *Dzögchen*, which in Tibetan means the Great Perfection, could I grasp the simple truth that lay behind the old man's smile. All is well, just as it is. To live this truth is to live beyond hope and fear.

DZÖGCHEN: THE GREAT PERFECTION

Dzögchen is the most elevated cycle of teachings in Tibet's ancient Bön tradition, providing the supreme and direct path to enlightenment. The Great Perfection refers to our true essence, which is perfect, complete and pure, free of karmic imprints and conditions.[84] Dzögchen teachings introduce us to our natural state of mind, which is our true essence. Research neurologist David Perlmutter and anthropologist and shaman Alberto Villoldo, who coauthored *Power Up Your Brain: Neuroscience of Enlightenment,* highlight Dzögchen as a practice that can alter the neural patterns of our distorted thoughts and beliefs, liberating us from the conditions that create hope and fear. In addition, when our state of mind is integrated and coherent, our physical body can become radiant and luminous.[85] When we can embody our true essence in life, Bön teaches that upon our death we can attain *jalus,* or *rainbow body,* the transformation of our physical body into pure light.

My introduction to Dzögchen came through meeting Tenzin Wangyal Rinpoche, a Tibetan Bön master and author of many books. Rinpoche, which is an honorary Tibetan term for 'precious teacher,' had just published a book on Dream Yoga, which he would be signing at a Los Angeles bookstore. The Bön lineage and the topic intrigued me, so I shifted my schedule to attend. Upon meeting Rinpoche, I felt a profound quickening deep within me, as if something dormant had sprung to life. Before leaving the bookstore I registered for Rinpoche's meditation training scheduled for the very next day. Although I had

---

84 Dzögchen is also considered the most dangerous path, because a misunderstanding of the view can lead to hubris and misguided behavior.
85 Perlmutter, D. & Villoldo, A. 2011.

been practicing mindfulness meditation for many years, this training would focus on Dzögchen, the most advanced meditation practice in the Bön tradition.

Arriving early, I entered the meditation hall and found a single empty seat across from Rinpoche. He greeted me with a warm smile, rekindling the resonance I felt the night before. The retreat began with the assembled students chanting the Guru Yoga, a Tibetan prayer that unifies the enlightened master with his students. Tears flowed down my cheeks. The long search for my spiritual teacher was at an end.

A few nights after returning home, I had a dream that affirmed my kinship with my chosen teacher and the Tibetan Bön lineage. In the dream, Rinpoche was giving me a teaching. His sole instruction was to point at the moon. I awoke perplexed but inspired. A month later, I traveled to Mexico City for another Bön retreat with Rinpoche. Early the first morning, while savoring huevos rancheros at a restaurant near the teaching center, I looked up to see Rinpoche walking towards my table. Surprised to find me in Mexico, he laughed and joined me for breakfast. As soon as he sat, I shared my dream with him. Rinpoche nodded, smiled and said, "Pointing to the moon is a direct transmission. That is a good sign." With complete trust and devotion, I immersed myself in the practices of Bön.

A year later, I was blessed to meet my soul mate, Tomás, a member of the sangha or spiritual community in Los Angeles. Our dance of getting to know each other began at a teaching by the Dalai Lama, and a few months later, when we connected, our souls collided and each of us saw a bright shooting star – one descended vertically and the other traced a horizontal path across the dark night sky. We took this as confirmation that Yeshe Walmo, the Wisdom Loving Mother and main protector of the Bön had answered our prayers for a conscious relationship.

***

For many years, I had followed the teachings of Siddhartha Gautama Buddha, but had not learned of Bön, the indigenous spiritual tradition of Tibet.

PART THREE THE FRUITION

According to tradition, the Bön lineage began approximately 18,000 years ago with the enlightened master, Tonpa Shenrab Miwoche. Like Siddhartha, Tonpa Shenrab Miwoche was born heir to a kingdom, trading his life of privilege for spiritual service and the pursuit of enlightenment. Tonpa Shenrab traveled to the land of Olmo Lungring, the ancient kingdom of Zhang Zhung, a vast empire encompassing all of Tibet as well as areas of Persia, Tajikistan, and China. Zhang Zhung's capital was Mount Kailash, the seat of Tibetan civilization.[86] Tibetans use the name Böd to identify their homeland, referencing their Bön spiritual heritage.

Bön wisdom and practices are conferred from master to student in an oral lineage that has endured unbroken since prehistory. Masters teach their students in a series of successive cycles known as nine ways or vehicles. One of these ways, termed the *causal vehicle*, focuses on shamanic practices that foster harmony with all of nature. The final way, Dzögchen, contains the secret practices that reveal the path to self-liberation. With the introduction of Buddhism, spreading from India to Tibet, Bön diminished in popularity. Despite the encroachment of Buddhism, Bön masters preserved their sacred lineage by continuing to practice and teach their ancient wisdom.[87]

Until the 1960's, Bön masters shared Dzögchen with carefully chosen advanced students. After the Tibetan uprising in 1959, many Tibetan monks fled to India and Nepal. Among the refugees were His Holiness, Lungtok Tenpai Nyima Rinpoche, the 33rd Abbot of Menri Monastery, and Yongdzin Tenzin Namdak Rinpoche, the most senior master, who the Dalai Lama deemed "a living treasure of Tibet." Together these two monks ensured that the Bön lineage would continue into the next century. Bön now flourishes, with teaching centers throughout the world.

***

---

86 [86]Norbu, Namkai. *Drung, Deu and Bön*, 1995.
87 Snellgrove D. *Nine Ways of Bön*, 1980.

I entered the sacred mandala of the Bön teachings with unwavering faith. After the initial retreats, I immersed myself in Rinpoche's book, *Wonders of the Natural Mind*, in which I learned of the self-arising wisdom of *Kunzhi*, the Base of All, a practice that dissolves hope and fear. I continued on my new spiritual path by learning a meditation practice called *zhiney*, or calm abiding, which requires students to focus on a sacred syllable or a point in space. After months of practicing zhiney and several other meditation techniques, I dove headlong into a weeklong retreat led by another Bön master.

The retreat center was located in an isolated desert near the border of Mexico. The main building had two stories, which included a large meeting room, a small kitchen, a single bathroom and an upstairs loft that served as dormitory for the forty participants. Before the retreat began I explored the surrounding landscape. I found an ancient rock formation from where I could gaze into the infinite desert sky. I had no idea that neither I nor the other participants would be permitted outside for the duration of the retreat.

The retreat commenced with a protection ritual that sealed and sanctified the space. The master announced that we must remain within the sacred boundary and maintain complete silence. Eye contact, looking out the windows, and bathing were forbidden. These restrictions served to direct our focus inward. Meals were light and nutritious. Our day began at 5 a.m., with long hours of zhiney practice lasting until 10 p.m. We spent our time on a cushion, gazing at an *Ah*, a sacred Tibetan symbol, posted on a stick at eye level. Blinking and swallowing were discouraged. Our master instructed us to let the 'waters' run down our cheeks and out of our mouths. To support the rigor of this practice we learned the nine breaths of purification and another practice, called *tsa lung*, to help stabilize the reactivity of our minds and bodies.[88]

Sitting upright for two-hour sessions, at times the pain could be overwhelming. Almost imperceptibly, I grew accustomed to the headaches, eyestrain, and muscle stiffness. During a particularly challenging afternoon my body started trembling. A tension shot from my head to my toes, filling my

---

88 For details, see Tenzin Wangyal Rinpoche, 2011.

body with an explosion of light. I collapsed, unable to move or speak. Earlier in the retreat our master had shared that this training would loosen and dissolve karmic imprints. Intense and unusual physical sensations, including paralysis, signaled that our practice was deepening.

Through consecutive days of the zhiney, free from distractions and responsibilities, I was learning to still my mind and to discharge dense energy from body. By retreat's end I felt lighter physically, emotionally, and spiritually. This experience became a cornerstone of my spiritual training, as each subsequent teaching brought me ever closer to my true essence and a connection with the infinite, boundless Source.

During a weeklong retreat at Serenity Ridge, Rinpoche's center in the Virginia countryside, I was introduced to a Dzögchen teaching called the Twenty-one Nails. Taking copious notes and earnestly struggling to comprehend the teaching, I had another breakthrough. During a meditation, everything froze, including my thoughts. I let go of my effort to try to understand. I could hear Rinpoche's voice, "Just as blood cannot be washed with blood, you cannot understand these teachings with conceptual mind." The words continued to loop through my mind until only their silent vibrations penetrated my awareness. A warm energy pierced the back of my head. Infinite space supplanted my ego identity mind, filling me with a radiant bliss. Again I could not move or speak. When I regained physical function, the bliss remained, lasting many hours. I heard people speak, but their words and my own thoughts dissolved before taking form. Unlike my first experience of cosmic consciousness, which catapulted my awareness outward into the vastness of space, abiding in my natural state of mind anchored me to the here and now. I was physically present, sensing everything, without a need to grasp anything.

Dzögchen became an integral part of my daily life, its teachings and practices nurturing an ongoing sense of awe and joy. Mindfulness meditation, the three pillars, and my Heart-Mind practice proved worthy and loyal companions on my journey of awakening. Yet, by discovering my spiritual teacher and lineage, I had found a new source of guidance and support. Armed with deepened awareness and courage I completed my doctorate in Transpersonal Psychology in 2002. *Unbinding the Soul,* left on the shelf for a decade, became my thesis.

GRACE AND DEATH

A well-known Tibetan story tells of a master lama who, upon hearing the news that his only son had died, became wracked with grief. Puzzled by the intensity of his teacher's emotion, a student asked, "Precious teacher, you taught us that all life is illusory. If this is true, why do you cry?" The lama, through his tears, calmly responded, "Oh yes, life is illusory. But my son was my greatest illusion." Although we may learn to discern our distorted and conditioned beliefs, we remain human and we experience the joys and the sorrows that life offers us. On our way back to wholeness we will not cease to feel. In Dzögchen there is no grasping or pushing away of anything, including deeply felt emotions. As the master lama in the story, I too had to face my greatest illusion. When my son Randy became ill, I was thrust into the abyss of the powerless mother who cannot stop her child from suffering. However, through my practice, I could return to the calm abiding of my natural state of mind. Nonetheless, I naïvely remained attached to the illusion that I had shed my fears of death and loss.

***

As I pressed further on my path, like the wise old man at the start of this chapter, I was faced with a number of 'perhaps' experiences. Loss returned as my teacher. Blessed with good health and a strong body, I was unprepared when I awoke one night drenched in sweat. Anxiety took hold and I began to tremble. Ants seemed to crawl beneath my skin. Terrified, I wanted to burst out screaming. I applied the three pillars and engaged the nine breaths of purification, cultivating enough inner space to avoid outright panic. Gradually, the shaking subsided, but I could not fall back to sleep. Despite two weeks of

PART THREE THE FRUITION

engaging the many practices I had learned, my anxiety and insomnia intensified. The illusion of good health crumbled, unearthing, yet again, my fear of powerlessness.

Menopause had begun. I had been preparing for this sacred rite of passage, which in many indigenous and ancient cultures symbolizes a woman's return to her powerful feminine wisdom. Having known the suffering of life's impermanence, I naïvely believed that menopause would be easy. I had gravely underestimated the power of hormones on my state of mind. Menopause's hormonal assault plunged me into a dark night of the soul, filled with destructive thoughts, including those of suicide. Prior to my awakening, this unexpected appearance of my shadow would have engulfed me. Now, however, I could ride the waves of my emotions without being dragged into an undercurrent of panic.

The challenging hormonal shifts of menopause peaked two years later with searing abdominal pain and two grapefruit-sized tumors. Faced with a potential cancer diagnosis, life once again hurled me into the abyss. During this time, I felt deeply rooted in the support of Great Mother. Trusting in Her love and wisdom, I surrendered to my sadness and fear. During the four months of uncertainty, I paused, taking a time out from my busy schedule. In that time another fear claimed my attention, a dread of being a burden to others. In losing my health, I unveiled deeply ingrained illusions – physical invincibility and total independence. Instead of pushing away these distorted beliefs, I continued to apply all that I had learned, deepening my ability to move beyond dualistic thinking, beyond my hope and my fear.

To physically prepare for my upcoming surgery I replaced my fast-paced aerobic workouts with daily walks and yoga. I also changed my diet. On the morning of the surgery I felt ready. As the anesthesiologist asked me to count backwards from 100, the room filled with a golden light. When I awoke, the surgeon greeted me with the good news that the tumors were benign. I reveled in gratitude and relief.

During my weeks of recovery, I was blessed with much help and support. Friends shared their gifts of healing, food, and good company, which I accepted, learning at last to be vulnerable and to receive. My mother and I, in our newfound intimacy, could shed our conditioned patterns and roles. One afternoon, wincing and struggling to sit up, I put aside my need to be strong. My mother, so long afraid of her own tenderness, held my head to her chest. I could hear her heartbeat as she rocked me and whispered, "You are still my *mei-mei,* my little one."

Although I could not reply, "Perhaps," when receiving the news of my initial diagnosis, learning to ask for help, receive support, and open my heart felt like my own unexpected herd of wild horses. I was closer to learning the old man's secret.

***

Two years later, my vibrant, independent mother suffered a debilitating stroke. It was my turn to hold her as she fought to recover the use of her right arm and leg. As the possibility of regaining her functioning dwindled, she became increasingly anxious and paranoid. One evening, she began screaming that soldiers were coming to take her away. Later, I realized my mother had conjured up traumatic memories of her escape during the Japanese invasion of Hong Kong. Psychotropic medication did much to soothe her dark thoughts, returning her ability to laugh and reminisce. Just as recovery seemed possible, another stroke, more massive than the first, left my mother in a coma.

I received the devastating news while presenting at an Energy Psychology conference in northern California. I rushed home to join my brother and sister at my mother's bedside in the intensive care unit. After a week-long vigil, my siblings and I made the heart-rending decision to stop the mechanical ventilator. Knowing my mother had little time, we transformed her hospital room into a shrine, filling the sterile wall space with family photos and images of the Blessed Mother and Jesus Christ. A recording of 'Ave Maria,' which she had always sung to us as children, became a lullaby that played throughout our visits.

PART THREE THE FRUITION

On a quiet evening, two weeks after taking her off the artificial breathing apparatus, with the hospital ward humming at a low din, I climbed into my mother's bed and held her close. I quickly entered another realm. There I encountered the formless image of my mother wandering aimlessly in the shadows. I engaged the vision, gently explaining to her the stroke and the subsequent coma. The vision turned and smiled, suddenly appearing as my mother's radiant, beautiful self. "Whenever you are ready, you may go," I whispered, now back in the hospital bed. My mother took a deep breath, and her body relaxed. My heart filled with a powerful wave of love. I lay with her until the nurse urged me to go home and rest. I kissed my mother gently, knowing this would be my final good-bye. Three hours later, my siblings and I met at the hospital entrance. The nurse had called to say my mother's breathing had slowed. We reached her bedside moments after she died. Feeling my mother's presence still in the room, I performed a silent ritual to guide her on her journey home.

Before the second stroke, my mother had asked me for help to release the anger she still harbored for my father. "I want to have peace," she said, "No more hatred in my heart." Now gazing at the body that remained in the bed, I knew my mother had left this life knowing forgiveness and grace. A few weeks later, I awoke in my own bed with a start. My mother had come to me in a dream, a smile on her face, ready to share the good news. "I am well. There are no bills to pay in heaven." I laughed recalling her lifelong worries about finances. My mother was assuring me that she had found peace.

Through my mother's death I came to know my gift for connecting with those that have died. I continued to encounter souls who sought guidance with transitioning to another realm or saying good-bye to loved ones. My raven ability to 'see in the dark' grew more powerful, revealing the inseparability of all that lives and all that dies.

***

My journey continued to bestow unexpected gifts and opportunities. In the months following my mother's passing, I received an invitation to teach in southern France. Rene, an eccentric acquaintance, wanted me to guide a group of students in accessing different realms of consciousness. Intrigued, I sought guidance in a shamanic journey. I traveled outside my body, landing at the threshold of an arched doorway, recessed in a steep mountainside. Coaxing the door ajar, I asked permission to enter. Sensing an invitation, I stepped inside. As my eyes adjusted to the dark, I found myself at the entrance of a large cave. Flickering lights and a curious musty aroma beckoned me into a nearby chamber. Before me stood a circle of strange-looking men adorned in ornate robes. A beam of golden light pierced the circle's center, revealing the form of a woman. Finding courage, I made my presence known by asking the woman her name. She answered with a single word, "Trust!" I awoke from the trance to find my body vibrating with the golden light. This strange journey seemed ample reason to make the trip to France. In addition to my therapy practice, I had begun teaching meditation and healing. Four of my students honored the call to 'trust' and joined me on the pilgrimage in October of 2007.

Arriving at the Cote d'Azur airport, the group received an enthusiastic welcome from our trip organizer and guide, Rene. His long hair, Tibetan silk shirt and knowing smile placed him out of time and hinted at our adventure to come. During a meal of steamed muscles and salad niçoise, Rene brought out a book of sacred sites in the local area. Flipping the pages, I opened to a photograph of the arched doorway I had entered in my trance. "Is there a cave behind this door?" I asked with a mix of hesitation and excitement. Rene nodded, bemused by my sudden animation. "This is the cave of Saint Tropheme, or Lazarus," he replied. "He was Mary Magdalene's brother." All at once, a golden light appeared. I knew instantly that the woman in my trance was Mary Magdalene herself. Before this trip, I had only known the Catholic account of Mary Magdalene as the penitent prostitute healed by Jesus. This pilgrimage marked the beginning of my relationship with this icon of sacred feminine wisdom. I felt ready to deepen my commitment to bringing Great Mother's message of unity and harmony out into the world.[89]

Returning from France I felt the pull to embody the wisdom of Great Mother. Still intent on following the Bön teachings, I found myself taking a detour, as I returned to my Christian roots. For three years I straddled the spiritual paths of East and West. While continuing to deepen my connection to Bön, I completed two more pilgrimages to southern France and immersed myself in Gnosticism and the Gospel of Mary Magdalene. I felt surprised to experience an effortless, 'pointing to the moon' understanding of the teachings, which felt familiar and seemed uncannily similar to Buddhism. As I completed my last pilgrimage to France, I received a request to teach mystic shamanic healing. My students included devout Catholics, Kabbalah students and Buddhist practitioners, manifesting the Great Mother's message of unity and harmony.

Simultaneously, I was invited to attend a gathering of a small group of Bön practitioners at Serenity Ridge, the beautiful sanctuary in Virginia established by Tenzin Wangyal Rinpoche. We were informed of a vision he had, to establish a secular program of meditation called 'The Three Doors,' in which the ancient Bön teachings would be distilled and shared with anyone who wants to find true happiness and peace of mind. According to Rinpoche, the three doors are *stillness of the body*, *silence of the speech* and *spaciousness of the mind*. By entering the three doors, one can discover our unchanging, ceaseless and blissful essence. Instead of looking for certainty and security externally, the realization of our true nature forms our inner refuge.[90]

As I began this three-year intensive training program, I entered into the mandala of my spiritual lineage and treasured the profound teachings that were beyond the separation of cultural and religious traditions. All of us students shared a connection to our true essence, which we learned to access through the three doors in order to transform our suffering, grasping minds.

---

89 Leloup, Jean Yves, (trans.) *The Gospel of Mary Magdalene*, 2002.
[87] For a more detailed account of this experience, see Chapter Eight, "Embodying Sacred Feminine and Magdalene Wisdom" in *Goddess Shift*, 2010.
90 www.the3doors.org

In 2010, I completed the 'Three Doors' training program, a charter member of the first graduating class. In order to deepen my practice, I felt drawn to enter the Tibetan forty-nine day solitary Dark Retreat, a practice for only the most advanced students who have proven their ability to mediate for long periods in total darkness. By accepting the call to Dark Retreat, I was also saying 'Yes!' to the call of Dark Mother, the divine feminine aspect who guards the mysteries of impermanence, uncertainty, chaos, and the never ending cycle of birth, death, and rebirth.

In July of 2010, my husband, Tomás, drove me out to Crestone, Colorado, where Rinpoche has a retreat center called Chamma Ling. Lying at the foot of the Sangre de Cristo Mountains in southern Colorado, it is a beautiful place to meditate in solitary retreat, either in daylight, sky-gazing, or in complete darkness, sealed into a comfortable cabin in the woods. Rooted in the refuge of my Bön spiritual masters and teachings as well as my faith in the Great Mother's love, I felt prepared for the lessons the retreat would impart. Crossing the threshold into the darkened cabin, I felt I was descending into the womb of the Dark Mother.

On my first night, I journeyed back in time and saw myself as a tiny fetus, fighting to survive, my heart stopping and restarting, and finally triumphing over my mother's attempts to terminate her pregnancy. Immersed in this vision, I began having a panic attack. I surrendered to the experience, and resorted to the many teachings and practices I had learned. I called on Dark Mother for her support and protection. My faith and my practice served me well. Forty-nine days later, I emerged reborn, having ventured into the outer reaches of the sacred, boundless and luminous space. My ordeal gifted me with the boon of expanded awareness. I could experience my everyday world with greater breadth and clarity. Physical boundaries seemed to dissolve and images and sounds saturated my senses in a way that was joyful rather than overwhelming. I now felt fully present, yet somehow unattached to daily activities or confined by normal human conditions.

PART THREE THE FRUITION

Seven weeks following my emergence from the dark retreat, my husband and I visited New Orleans, where he was giving a paper at the annual meeting of the American Anthropological Association. New Orleans is a magical place, a crucible for the dark mysteries of colliding traditions. While wandering in the French Quarter, we discovered an intriguing museum and shop, which was past 'closing time,' but the door was unlocked so we entered. Inside, there was a beautiful old Haitian woman, dressed in white, sitting by the checkout stand. Not recognizing her immediately, we continued browsing the museum and bookstore and she left, escorted by a small entourage. I spotted a book on the shelf and said, "Look, Tomás, Mama Lola! Isn't that the book you used for one of you classes?" Overhearing me, one of the clerks came up and said, "That was Mama Lola who was just here! Would you like to meet her?" "Certainly," I said, and we were taken outside and introduced to the Vodou priestess of Brooklyn.[91] We hugged and talked for a minute, and then as I was saying good-bye to Mama Lola, one of her assistants whispered into my ear, "Come to the shop tomorrow at one, and you can have a reading."

The next day, we arrived at the appointed hour and I sat down at a table, across from Mama Lola. She pulled out a regular pack of playing cards and began shuffling the deck. I was greatly taken with her energy and the wisdom that shone in her smiling eyes. She asked me to cut the deck, and then she gently laid out all the cards on the table. I held my breath as she looked at the cards. There was a moment of silence. She looked up at me with a puzzled expression and then looked down at the cards in front of her. Was something wrong? She leaned in close and inquired, "Why did you want a reading?"

I didn't know how to respond to this question. She continued, "You don't need a reading." I was stunned. Then she asked another strange question, "Tell me, why do the spirits love you so much?" Amused by my puzzled expression, Mama Lola began to laugh and said, "You are surrounded by such light, dear one." She pointed out that my signifying card was right next to the card that

---

91 Brown, K.M. *Mama Lola: A Vodou Priestess in Brooklyn*, 2001.

represents Dambala, the highest Vodou god, and that all of the spirit protectors were surrounding me.

Taking my hand, she smiled broadly and proclaimed, "You are my sister. There is nothing I can teach you. In fact, you could be teaching me." Though surprised by the recognition of this holy woman, I humbly accepted her blessing and gave her a big hug of appreciation.

A SOUL UNBOUND

As I reflect back on my six-decade journey from dutiful, fearful daughter to mystic shaman healer, I am humbled and amazed by the depth and breadth of my transformation. Burdened by the skepticism and doubt arising from my egoic self, I often wondered if I had lost my mind. Persevering, I learned to trust, recognizing and accepting the support, lessons, and opportunities that seemed to magically appear on my path. Wise teachers and powerful practices led me to new thresholds of divine consciousness, whose pure vibration continued to dissolve the fear-based illusions that separated me from my true nature. Gary's suicide threw open the portal to my awakening, shattered my conditioned identity and hurtled me on a quest into the dark realms of the unknown. Finding my footing, I navigated a labyrinth of ordeals and blessings, charting a path that led beyond dualistic thinking, beyond hope and fear and into the light of higher awareness.

Along the way, I encountered the many faces of my shadow. Although terrifying and painful, acknowledging and accepting my vulnerability, rage, and shame yielded invaluable insights. By accepting and integrating these previously rejected parts of myself, I continued learning to shed reactive and habitual patterns of thinking, feeling and behaving. Opening to new and higher levels of consciousness, I could also open myself to new levels of personal intimacy. I am now blessed to share the journey with my soul mate and fellow Bön practitioner, Tomás. Our relationship is yet another portal, reflecting deeper layer of fears, judgments, attachments and doubts. Despite the enduring pull of my pain story, I keep returning to my heart-mind, dissolving into the inner refuge of unbounded space, infinite radiance and the all-encompassing love that is my true essence.

My love for Randy and Jennifer, of course, remains boundless and abiding. Having embraced that part of me that is the powerless and imperfect mother, I can love my children without the fears and attachments that plagued their earlier years. I remain awed by the depth of their awareness, their ability to ride the waves of their emotions, and their resilience in the face of devastating trauma. Despite the challenges they endured having a single mother who was at times overwhelmed and unavailable, they *know* my love and have learned to celebrate and accept my gifts and failings. In so doing, I wish that they in turn can love and accept their own humanness, bringing light to their shadow and kindling their inner radiance.

I continue in my calling to heal others and myself and to be a vessel of the sacred feminine wisdom. My roles as student, seeker, practitioner, healer and teacher deepen and expand as I move further on my journey. In 2011, my root teacher, Tenzin Wangyal Rinpoche, bestowed me the highest honor by entrusting me to be one of the teachers for his 'Three Doors Academy.' I am profoundly humbled to be a vessel of Light and given the opportunity to share this awakening with others.

The dance of awareness is ongoing, as is the quest for transformation and wholeness. Some of you may be just peeking through a portal, uncertain of how to step across the threshold. For others, your initiation may have occurred long ago. Each of us has the ability to unbind our souls, to release our conditioned egoic identity to reveal our true nature, our divine essence. If we open ourselves to receiving support and guidance, we can understand our heartbreaks, disappointments and tragedies as sacred wounds that crack us open, giving space to the light and transforming our crises into loving wisdom.

As my Tibetan Bonpo masters say, "E Ma Ho. How marvelous!"

May our suffering be a gift of awakening through compassion!

APPENDIX ONE – THE TRIUNE BRAIN

The neuroscientist Paul D. Maclean developed the model of the Triune Brain. The following outline describes the developmental phase, location, and functions of each section of the Triune Brain.

REPTILIAN BRAIN: (SENSORY-MOTOR)

DEVELOPMENTAL PHASE: First trimester in utero.
LOCATION: Brainstem.
FUNCTIONS:
- Receives information via the body and five senses.
- Mediates basic physiological states including breathing, temperature regulation, and heart rate.
- Responds via Fight-Flight-or-Freeze response, our reflexive survival instinct.

MIDBRAIN: LIMBIC REGION: (EMOTIONAL-COGNITIVE)

DEVELOPMENTAL PHASE: Second trimester in utero.
LOCATION: Rests on top of the brain stem.
FUNCTIONS:
- Generates our emotions.

- Mediates meaning appraisal, social cognition, motivation and goal-directed behavior.
- Regulates endocrine and immune systems.
- Promotes our ability to bond and nurture.
- Affects how memories are recorded and retrieved via regulation of emotional intensity.
- Influences our values, beliefs, identity and self-awareness.

NEOCORTEX OR CEREBRAL CORTEX: (HIGHER FUNCTONS)

DEVELOPMENTAL PHASE: Begins to develop near the end of the second trimester.

LOCATION: Top and sides of the visible brain. Makes up the largest section of the brain.

FUNCTIONS:
- Mediates the most complex functions of the brain including perception, reasoning, and abstract thought.
- The left hemisphere is responsible for logic, reason, communication, and language.
- The right hemisphere is responsible for creativity, intuition, and empathy.

PREFRONTAL CORTEX: (MEDIATES AND INTEGRATES)

DEVELOPMENTAL PHASE: Begins to develop after birth and continues to mature until we reach our 20's. Our environment and relationships affect its development.

LOCATION: The front portion of the neocortex.

FUNCTIONS:
- Responsible for intelligence and problem solving capabilities.

- Allows flexibility and adaptability of emotions in response to experiences, promoting complex decision making.
- Links current experience with past memories.
- Connects with the limbic region of the brain to balance the autonomic nervous system, responsible for the body's arousal and relaxation responses.

APPENDIX TWO - THE NINE DOMAINS OF INTEGRATION

Dr. Dan Siegel defines *mind* as an embodied and relational process that regulates a flow of energy and information. The brain has distinct anatomical areas, each with its specialized function. When the specialized areas of the brain are linked through a cohesive neural network, they can operate as a unified system. The energy and information of *mind* flow freely through this unified system to create an *integrated state of mind*, which allows us to experience our thoughts and emotions as flexible, adaptive, coherent, energized, and stable (FACES). Siegel asserts varying types of neurobiological integration, which he terms 'The Nine Domains of Integration.'

The Heart-Mind Mediation Process helps us to strengthen the connections within all nine domains so we can cultivate our compassionate witness and experience FACES thinking and feeling.

1. *consciousness* – The awareness of what we experience and what we know. This allows us to recognize our habitual reactive patterns so we can choose how we will respond.
2. *horizontal* – The connection between the left and right hemispheres of the brain. This promotes an expanded and balanced perspective of our experience. The left hemisphere is responsible for thought that is linear,

logical, and literal. The right hemisphere is responsible for thought that is symbolic, imaginal, holistic, non-verbal, and emotional.
3. *vertical* – The connections that move between the neocortex, through the lower portions of the brain, along the spinal cord and into the peripheral nervous system. This allows us to perceive the information that comes through our senses, giving us full body awareness.
4. *memory* – The integration of *explicit* memory [information we consciously attempt to retrieve] and *implicit* memory [information that arises unconsciously without effort or will].
5. *narrative* – The weaving of episodic autobiographical memories to create our personal story. This allows us to cultivate our compassionate witness who observes our story without judgment.
6. *state* – The simultaneous management of differing and/or conflicting states of mind such as anxiety with contentment, judgment with acceptance, and despair with joy.
7. *temporal* – The connection of our personal narrative with time. This promotes our awareness and acceptance of uncertainty, impermanence, and death.
8. *interpersonal* – The supportive interactions we have with others. Healthy relationships and attachments enhance the complexity of neural connections in the brain.
9. *transpirational* – The awareness of our physical and personal identity extending beyond the boundaries of time and space. We feel an interconnection with all that is, all that was, and all that will be in the future. We exist as part of a universal whole.

REFERENCES

Axline, V. *Dibs In Search of Self.* New York: Ballatine Books, 1964

Blakeslee, S. *The Body Has a Mind of Its Own.* Random House, 2007

Bohm, D. *Wholeness and the Implicate Order.* London: Routledge, 1980

Bowlby, J. *Attachment and Loss.* Basic Books, 1983

Brown, K.M. *Mama Lola: A Vodou Priestess in Brooklyn.* University of California Press, 2001

Burke, R. *Cosmic Consciousness.* Martino Fine Books, 2010, reprint of 1905

Cameron, E. *Negotiating Gender: Initiation Arts of Mwadi and Mukanda.* University of California, Los Angeles, Doctoral Thesis, 1995

Campbell, J. *The Power of Myth.* Anchor, 1991

Cortright, B. *Psychotherapy and Spirit.* State University of New York Press, 1997

Dalai Lama *My Life In Forbidden Lhasa.* National Geographic, 1955

Dalai Lama. *Becoming Enlightened.* Atria Books, 2009

Davidson, R. *The Emotional Life of your Brain.* Plume, 2012

Dossey, Larry. *Recovering the Soul.* Bantam Books, New York, 1989

Ecker, B. *Unlocking the Emotional Brain.* London: Routledge, 2012

Feinstein, D., Eden, D. & Craig, P. *The Promise of Energy Psychology,* 2005

Eliade, M. *Shamanism: Archaic Techniques of Ecstasy.* London: Routledge and Kegan Paul, 1964

Gallo, F. *Energy Tapping for Trauma.* New Harbinger Publication Inc. 2007

Gilbert P. *Compassion: Conceptualizations, Research and Use in Psychotherapy*. London: Routledge, 2005

Gilbert, P. *A Compassionate Mind*. New Harbinger Publications, 2010

Grof, S. *The Cosmic Game*, State University of New York Press, 1998

Hahn, Thich Nhat. *Peace is Every Step*. Bantam, 1992

Ho, M.W. *Towards a New Ethics of Science*. Institute of Science in Society and Biology, 2000

Ho, M.W. *The Rainbow and the Worm*. World Scientific Publishing Co, Singapore, 2008

Hunt, V. *An Infinite Mind*. Malibu Publishing Co., 1996

Jaffe, A. *Memories, Dreams and Reflection*. London, 1964

James, W. *The Varieties of Religious Experience*. New York: Longmans, 1902

Jung, C.G. *Modern Man in Search of a Soul*. Harcourt Harvest, 1955, original print 1933

Jung, C.G. *Collected Works of C.G. Jung*. Princeton University Press, Bollingen Series, 1961

Jung, C.G. *Analytical Psychology: Its Theory and Practise*. London: Routledge & K. Paul, 1968

Kabat-Zinn, J. & Brantley, J. *Calming Your Anxious Mind*. New Harbinger Publications 2003

Kendall, E. *In Search of Memory*. W. W. Norton & Co., 2007

Kornfield, Jack. *Meditation for Beginners*. Sounds True, 2008

Kohut, H. *The Analysis of the Self*. University of Chicago Press, 1971

Leloup, Jean Yves (trans). *The Gospel of Mary Magdalene*. Vermont: Inner Traditions, 2002

Lee, B.R. (anthology), edited by Marohn, S. *Goddess Shift*. Elite Books, 2010

Lipton, Bruce. *The Biology of Belief*. Mountain of Love/Elite Books, 2005

Lutz, Dunne, & Davidson. *Handbook of Consciousness*. Cambridge University Press, 2007

Maslow, A. *Toward a Psychology of Being* Van Nostrand, 1968

Miller, A. *For Your Own Good* New York: Farrar-Straus-Giroux, 1983

REFERENCES

Mindell, A. *Quantum Mind*. Lao Tse Press, 2000

Namkai Norbu Rinpoche. *Drung, Deu and Bön*. Ltwa., 1995

Newberg, A. *The Metaphysical Mind*. Create Space, 2013

Ogden, P. *Trauma and the Body*. W. W. Norton & Co., 2006

Palmer, M. *Kuan Yin Chronicles*. Hampton Roads Pub Co., 2009

Perera. S. *Descent to the Goddess*. Inner City Books, 1981

Perlmutter, D. & Villodo, A. *Power up your Brain*. Hay House, 2012

Pert, C. *The Molecules of Emotions*. Simon and Schuster, 1997

Rama, Ballentine, & Hymes, *Science of Breath*. Himalayan Institute Press, 2007

Shinoda Bolen, J. *The Goddesses in Every Woman*. Harper & Row, 1984

Shore, A. *Affect Dysregulation and Disorders of the Self*. W.W. Norton & Co., 1994

Schore, A. *Affect Regulation and the Origin of the Self*. W.W. Norton & Co., 1994

Siegel, D. *The Developing Mind*. Guilford Press, 1999

The Mindful Brain. W.W. Norton & Co., 2007

Mindsight. Bantam, 2010

Snellgrove D. *Nine Ways of Bön*. Great Eastern Book Co., 1980

Trungpa, C. *Cutting Through Spiritual Materialism*. Shambhala Publications Inc., 1986

Singer, J. *Boundaries of the Soul*. Doubleday, 1972

Wangyal, T. *Wonders of the Natural Mind*. Snow Lion, 1993

Wangyal, T. *Awakening the Sacred Body*. Hay House, 2011

Wilber, K. *A Theory of Everything*. Shambhala Publications Inc., 2001

Woodman, M. *Conscious Femininity*. Inner City Books, 1993

Wolff, Fred. A. *Mind into Matter*. Moment Point Press Inc., 2000

Zukav, Gary. *The Seat of the Soul*. Simon & Schuster Inc., 1990

INDEX

adaptation 7, 62
as it is 63, 69
attachment 13, 30-31, 94, 145,181, 188
attuning 91, 132-133
awakening 5, 13, 16, 48, 114, 131, 146
awareness xv-xvi, xxii, 5, 8, 22, 63, 80, 98, 109, 122-123, 128-132, 144
beginner's mind 70, 76
bliss xviii, 65, 67-69, 144, 157, 171
Bön xx, 131, 167-170
brain 24, 29-36
Buddha 11, 13, 49, 80, 93, 127
    ,(teachings) 13, 93
calm abiding 76, 170
caregivers 20, 31
chaos 6, 106
cells 23-24, 35, 83-84, 120, 122
compassion xxii, 5, 79, 80-85, 118, 132, 134, 140
compassionate awareness xvi, 5, 114, 119, 188
cosmic consciousness 68-69, 146
crisis xvi, xxiii, 4-10, 31, 63-64, 105,
    (Chinese symbol) 6
Dalai Lama 80, 93-94, 146

disintegration 111
dukkha ('dissatisfaction') 13, 49
Dzögchen 167-169, 171
electromagnetic energy 83, 120, 122, 131
emotions 31, 33, 36, 84, 99, 105-107, 119-124, 187
energy xxii, 35, 83, 92, 106, 120-124, 133, 187
fight-flight-freeze response 33, 183
heart 75, 83-87, 91, 120
Heart-Mind Transformation 127-130
imprints 167, 171
initiation 8-9, 154
integration 7, 33, 36-37, 187
interconnectedness 92, 121, 143
IPNB (interpersonal neurobiology) 34
ipseity 63
listen 89, 91,
 (Chinese character) 90
meditation 12, 64, 94, 97-100, 170-171
memory 30, 36, 120, 188
mind 34-37
 (definition of) 35
neural plasticity 31, 98
neurobiology 62
perception 19, 31, 36, 144
perspective 5, 7, 49, 109
refuge 75-76, 177
resilience 8
samsara 14, 49
self 19, 23, 87, 92, 106
Siddhartha Gautama 11, 168
siddhi 93, 146

soul xxi-xxiii, 180
suffering xv, 12-13, 49, 80, 93-95
    (forbidden) 41, 111
Tenzin Wangyal Rinpoche 89, 91, 131, 165, 167, 170-171, 177
Truths (4 Noble) 13, 93
wisdom 8, 10, 81, 85-86, 90, 105, 170,
    (feminine) 149

Made in the USA
San Bernardino, CA
22 June 2015